Contents

Pop Fiction

The Song in Cinema

Edited by Steve Lannin and Matthew Caley

intellect™

This book is dedicated to the research staff at the School of Art and Design, the University of Wolverhampton, especially Mathew Cornford without whose support it would not have been possible.

Many thanks to the Graphic Communications team, particularly George Marks.

First Published in the UK in 2005 by

Intellect Books, PO Box 862, Bristol BS99 1DE, UK

First Published in the USA in 2005 by

Intellect Books, ISBS, 920 NE 58th Ave. Suite 300, Portland, Oregon 97213-3786, USA

Copyright ©2005 Intellect Ltd

A catalogue record for this book is available from the British Library

ISBN 1-84150-078-X

Cover Design: Lannin/Caley/Solomons

Copy Editor: Julie Strudwick

Printed in Great Britain by Cromwell Press Limited, Trowbridge, Wiltshire.

Foreword

Film music studies has been undergoing what might be thought of as a naissance - the first significant period of fertility - in the past few years. There is, undoubtedly, a case to be made that there was an early flourishing of works at the time of the birth of sound on film, with works such as Leonid Sabaneev's 1935 Music for the Films *and Kurt London's 1936* Film Music, *for example. But those works were not speaking to each other, and thus, to my mind, they did not constitute a field or an object of study. One might also argue that the current blossoming actually begin in the late 80's and early 90's, with* Unheard Melodies *(Gorbman, 1987),* Settling the Score *(Kalinak, 1992), and* Strains of Utopia *(Flinn, 1992). And in some ways, that's clearly true. But it took most of the 1990s for that opening to really take root.*

The past few years, however, have heard an explosion of work. Suddenly, there are books like Martin Marks Music and the Silent Film, *anthologies like* Soundtrack Available *and* Music and the Cinema, *articles in film and music journals, and conference panels and even entire conferences. And what that means, of course, is that as a community of scholars we can begin asking much more interesting, detailed questions. That's where this present volume comes in.*

Unlike any other collection, all of the essays here focus on a single song and its place in a single film. Perhaps this sounds like an obvious approach. But in fact, most work on film music (with a few significant exceptions) has accepted the received notion that pre-existing songs do not play significant roles in the film that houses them. Pop Fiction *does away with that notion once and for all. In all 12 essays, these authors make compelling cases that the films in question would be markedly different were it not for the song they discuss.*

In some ways, the delight of this volume is the wide range of theoretical and disciplinary approaches to the topic. Several essays use psychoanalytic paradigms. For example, in Always Blue: Chet Baker's Voice, *John Roberts focuses on the intersections of Chet Baker's biography and the grain of his voice to argue that while both his addition and his vocal limitations have been used to dismiss Baker as a vocalist, other interpretations are possible. Roberts suggests that Baker offers what psychoanalytic theorists call "the good voice" of the mother, creating a "sonorous envelope" in which the listening subject can bask. Thus, Baker's performance of* Always Blue, *written for him by Elvis Costello, in* Let's Get Lost, *Bruce Weber's 1986 documentary biography of Baker, offers a hauntingly beautiful space of pleasure.*

In "Music, Masculinity and Membership," Ian Inglis discusses Frankie Valli's Can't Take My Eyes off of You *in Michael Cimino's 1978* The Deer Hunter, *showing how the careful placement of a song can create multiple layers of meaning. Inglis argues that, in this case, the song opens threads of homosociality and homoeroticism that intersect with and alter the film's nationalist discourse. Phil Powrie, too, considers a homosocial homoerotic text; this time, it's Quentin Tarantino's* Reservoir Dogs. *While most commentators heard Stealer's Wheel's* Stuck in the Middle with You *as a form of ironic counterpoint to the violence of the scene in which it appears, Powrie argues compellingly that it opens a sado-masochistic space of anal abjection, "a viewing-hearing position in which disgust and desire reinforce each other and guarantee the disintegrated integrity of our viewing and hearing experience."*

Powrie's work opens the question of the relationship of audition to spectatorship, a theme taken up by many of the volumes authors. Through deft uses of Marxist and poststructuralist theory, Dave Beech shows how the lyrics of Leonard Cohen's I'm Your Man *provide a point of entry into Nanni Moretti's challenging politics of artist and audience in* Dear Diary. *In Beech's analysis, we the audience are positioned by* Dear Diary *as devoted lovers, inhabiting a Derridian complex of hospitality and its hostility within.*

Heavy Rotation, Matthew Caley's essay, treats the poetic relations produced among image, text and sound by the placement of The Doors' The End *in* Apocalypse Now's *opening sequence. Playing on the pun of revolution in the triangulation of the ceiling fan, the helicopter blades, and the song's lyrics, Caley argues that this poetic moment lightens the heavy burden of the film's pessimistic vision.*

[6]

Lannin's own contribution, Fluid Figures: How To See Ghosts, offers a novel and unexpected approach to the place of the Righteous Brothers cover of Unchained Melody *in* Ghost. *Through the prism of gestalt psychology, he suggests that the shape of the song and the shape of the film as a whole makes possible a wide range of entry points, creating a much richer and more complex film than might at first be seen and heard.*

In his detailed analysis of both the music of Lou Reed's Perfect Day *and its relationship to the visual images in one sequence of* Trainspotting, *Miguel Mera treats audition and spectatorship. He does an excellent job of showing how musical, including harmonic, structures make meaning. He argues, for example, that the alternation between B-flat major in the chorus and b-flat minor in the verse produces a "bittersweet personification of the pleasure/pain concept." Such careful musical analysis will, I believe, be central to the future of film music studies.*

From a similar disciplinary perspective, Robynn Stillwell introduces the notion of "clean reading" to mean both a stable reading, on the one hand, and a reading free from contamination on the other. She argues that the presence of Phil Collins' In The Air Tonight *in* Risky Business *is unclean in two senses-slippery within the film and problematized by its many uses after the film's release-and thereby offers more interesting interpretive possibilities.*

Both Mera and Stillwell engage another thread that runs throughout the volume, and that is the question of intertextuality. The use of a Guns 'n' Roses cover version of Live and Let Die *in* Grosse Pointe Blank *provides Jeff Smith with an opportunity to consider intriguing questions about covers, intertextuality and sound space in a moment of film music that at first hearing is neither complicated nor noteworthy. Smith's analysis pointedly suggests that we overlook such songs at deep cost to our understanding.*

Elizabeth Hirschman sees a correlation between the song Man of Constant Sorrow *in* Oh Brother, Where Art Thou *and the Coen brothers Jewish identity, and a further connection between their Jewishness and the film's stereotypical portrayal of the South, using other filmic representations of the South as touchstones in her analysis. Morris Holbrook argues for the importance of the term "ambidiegesis," which he has coined to mean a performance that serves dramatic and/or character development, in his analysis of* My Funny Valentine *in both* The Fabulous Baker Boys *and* The Talented Mr. Ripley. *He uses both the term and his readings of the song's uses in the two films to take issue with the notion that what many theorists have termed diegetic music has more and different narrative possibilities than most writers suggest. David Toop, known as both a music writer and sound artist, contributes an evocative consideration of the place of Massive Attack's* Karmacoma *in Wong Kar-Wai's 1995* Fallen Angels. *The song serves the film elegantly, he suggests; it's multiplicity and complexity both share and articulate the film's decentered vision.*

[7]

Pop Fiction *is an important contribution to film music studies; it offers a view of the field as it is practiced now. But more than that, it offers a glimpse of things to come: more detailed and focused studies on the one hand (as in the volume's theme of the place of a particular song in a particular film), and more wide-ranging on the other (as can be seen from the invocations of, e.g., gestalt psychology, Derrida, and Ezra Pound). And if this is the future of film music studies, I can't wait.*

Anahid Kassabian, New York, 2003

Introduction

Steve Lannin and Matthew Caley

Popular Music is objectively untrue and helps to maim the consciousness of those exposed to
it, however hard the individual crippling effects may be to measure.

(Adorno, 1962)

*Renton, junkie-skinhead, is racing down an Edinburgh street, hotly pursued by police,
accompanied by the opening bars of Iggy Pop's* Lust For Life, *together with his own voice-over
reciting an ironic consumerist litany - 'choose a job etc.'. Analysing the opening sequence to
Danny Boyle's* Trainspotting, 1996 *(from Irving Welsh's novel) we might, at first order
significance, consider it a fine, pulsing, visceral and arresting (sic) opening - perfectly matching
the beat of the song. We could go on to consider how the use of the song brings Mr Osterberg's
own mythology of drug-addiction, mental breakdown, violence and genuine outsider status to
bear upon the junkie's reality. Pop's overtly sexual image - no article about him is complete
without speculating on how 'well-hung' he is - links to the junkie's declaration that a 'hit' is 'better
than any meat-injection' - developing a neatly ironic play around the needle/phallus comparison
and the fact that heroin nullifies sexual desire. This is merely the beginning of a journey of
association, demonstrating one role in one cinematic situation.*

Between Adorno and Trainspotting *we can begin to perceive the drug connotations that a pop
song may attract - but this leads to the more fundamental question: What does it mean to place
a popular song into a cinematic situation? Is it like a pharmaceutical product, affecting the
audience with an invisible but undeniable force of experience? (with or without maiming). Like the
drug, an audience won't always notice a familiar tune until the product is completely ingested,
humming a refrain whilst exiting the theatre. Or more similar to placing a famous actor on the
screen, or positioning the movie action in a particular locale - perhaps near to a famous landmark,
both capitalising (sic) on associated qualities?*

*Unlike a landmark, panacea or celebrity the pop song's make up is most similar to film itself,
created from the same series of components - image, text, sound - a deconstruction of which
shows how these common elements might usefully interact - aurally, conceptually and viscerally.
In this regard the question may legitimately be asked - surely a pop song has text (lyric/title) and
sound (music/voice) but how does it have 'image'? The answer is that 'image' in a pop song
might be the 'images' conjured by the lyrics, its iconic singer(s), its record-sleeve, the ubiquitous
accompanying video-clip, its previous use in adverts or the 'dream-images' it conjures up for the*

[9]

individual or collective consciousness - in other terms its hinterland of visual associations. The pop song adds its own suite of meanings to a films, and how this heady mix is managed is of primary importance to whether the film succeeds in its endeavours - be they commercial, creative or political.

(A songs on-screen action can be invisible or obvious and deliberate, it can transform and intensify any screen moment. It has multifarious abilities to extend the screen through affective and subjective dimensions, with limitless transcendence of the image. Manipulating, yes. Crippling, no.

Historically (especially in comparison to the literary and visual aspect) there was little written about cinematic sound until very recently. Although early works about Composing for the Films (Adorno & Eisler, 1947) do exist, the diffidence to the popular is transparent, with concessions viewed as pandering to the 'oppressive culture industry'. Adorno ensured that the popular song was also academically discredited, most notably in his Introduction to the Semiology of Music (1962), see the introductory quote.

Many important essays of cinematic dissection have previously failed to locate the position of an audio aspect at all. Laura Mulvey's Visual Pleasure and Narrative Cinema (1975) excludes any notion of sound from her psychological subject formation theory, (later rectified by Kaja Silverman for The Acoustic Mirror (1988)). This remained true, despite the attempts by Yale French Studies to spark debate, until the intervention of Weis, Belton, Altman and more especially Gorbman and Chion during the latter 1980s. Although the production work by sound and film editor Walter Murch, (examples of which are discussed in essays by both the editors), inspired much of the writing that followed.

Anahid Kassabian's excellent Hearing Film (2001) opens by summarising the literature that concerns musical meaning. She refers to scholars like Bazelon (and Adorno again) who insist that music only gains meaning through the bad listening habits of the participant. This is contrasted with reference to Unheard Melodies (1987) by Gorbman, clearly communicating the meaningful affect of music on a film scene, when she 'commutates' a sequence from Jules et Jim, envisaging different scorings and the likely changes of signification.

Popular music studies initiated by Simon Firth et al., began to consider the sociological effect/affects of the burgeoning music video industries on youth culture in Sound and Vision (1993), with 'youth films' given mention, but little analysis. However, the pop song only began to establish respectability as an important aspect in cinema through the interventions of books like The Celluloid Jukebox (1995), a thematic celebration of pop music's historically expanding influence on the big screen medium. One of its authors, David Toop, the curator of Britain's largest Sound Art exhibition at the Hayward in 2000, and a real pop musician to boot, here tracks a fairly obscure remix of Massive Attack's inner-city angst hit Karmacoma, as it pits dub-sounds against what he dubs dub camerawork through a dialogue free nightscape in Wong Kar Wai's Fallen Angels. His argument is that interplay between image and abstract sound is in fact dialogue. A new type of dialogue we are only just opening our eyes and ears to.

Chronologically, Jeff Smiths Sounds of Commerce (1998) is the next important step for the field, examining particular pop songs in film (mostly from the sixties), some in great detail rather than as a series of connected themes. His approach to economic and cultural aspects of the film-song, parallel works by Holbrook and Hirschmann, who in the Semiotics of Consumption (1993), interpret films as signifiers of marketing behaviour and sociological force, of which the pop song is another conspicuous example. In this volume Smith discusses how the Bond song Live and Let Die can associate itself with a new film character and provide a means of comedic parallel. He demonstrates how the song presents contrasted views of a similar profession by signalling its original role. However, Smith's writing has previously generated controversy, some musicologists (like Miguel Mera), taking exception to the deconstruction of this art form when using purely commercial imperatives. Here the pop song can become the location for a set of discourses about consumption. Taking our previous example of Lust for Life in Trainspotting where the song interacts with the consumerist litany at a deeper level, via the repeated use of the word 'choose' - the mantra of selling - emphasising the repeated use of the word 'life' in the song like a secularised/demonised-gospel call and response. The 'lust' of the song's title becomes the Lacanian notion of 'desire' - spurred by 'lack' - which can 'fix' itself on anything without hierarchy: a loved one, the craving for a cigarette, a 70s song. The point here is that there is no choice or alternative outside of the all-pervading terms of Late Capitalism unless as an abject one. This is one possible reading of the movie, supported from its opening by the song compilation, and that it's subject is not about heroin addition per se, but the use of heroin addiction as a metaphor for what Baudrillard calls the 'the pathological nature of consumption'. Mera's chapter, considering another 'drug-related' song Perfect Day from Trainspotting, uncovers the dualism within the song's harmonic construction and how this supports the film's cinematic content, utilising this opportunity to propose a more balanced approach to film/music scholarship.

When considering the scope of this project, Moulin Rouge, a contemporary Musical, obviously made a powerful claim for inclusion and was suggested by several of our authors. However this forced us to reflect, thinking backwards over twenty-five years from Baz Lurmann's extravaganza, upon an era characterised by the absence of this genre's commercial success, and why the Musical had withered in popularity, as the complied soundtrack became an increasingly popular device. (Strangely Altman's books on the musical appear just as this happens). Perhaps it compared unfavourably against the rise of the Pop Promo, whose fantasies were more expansive, expensive, faster cut and over in three minutes. (The pop video more than any other format relies heavily on what Chion (1994) calls 'Synchresis', the brains desire to match synch points in music to any visual material within its proximity). During the 1980s it is also possible to envisage the compiled score as replacing the need for the Musical's song and dance elements, in a period where fantasy was a way of life, not a change of scene. Post-modernism insisted on no longer attending the fantasy celebration, but becoming it. The film became an extension of life and both were expected to move to the beat of a similarly compiled score.

All of these considerations suggested a wider than anticipated division between the former genre and the new music-lead formats, one that deserved acknowledgement. The final factor that prompted excluding this film category from the book is that the diegesis of a popular song in a musical is very different from any other cinema. Normally a song is either heard (diegetic) or unheard (non-diegetic) by a cinematic character. In the musical there is a 'super-diegetic' situation where the character sings diegetically and an orchestra plays in a state of diegetic ambiguity. More importantly this construction, which enables ordinary human beings to become 'super-human' (hundreds dancing in coordination, time stopping, traffic stopping, etc.), defines a new form of reality, and is radically different to incorporating a song into a film, whether performed or merely compiled. One exception we allowed is discussed by Holbrook, taking liberties with the diegetic extremes, and exampling My Funny Valentine from The Fabulous Baker Boys, to reconstitute the Musical, in a new form, for an older market.

[12]

Revisiting the earlier theme of celebrity, a cult that has changed little since a face, especially a film star's, became the size of a house. The pop song, like the TV luminary, achieves size in the public consciousness via repetition, where vast amounts of time equate to filling a huge visual space. Warhol, the king of repetition, when questioned in his pre-Factory studio about why he constantly replayed one pop song, insisted that he would listen until he understood it. Warhol, of course, was never one to invite guests to his home.

Curator and contemporary art commentator, Dave Beech, passionately argues for cinema to give us a more humble welcome. His co-opting of Derrida's notion of the hostility within hospitality when referring to Moretti's Dear Diary is a call for a more human-scale cinema animated by love. Leonard Cohen's I'm Your Man in this context is a theme-tune for both this notion and the film being itself a plea for a selfless, almost self-abnegating love. Under Beech's formulation, most Hollywood produce is the smiling host that loathes the guest.

From similar background (but with longer pedigree), John Robert's fascination with the melancholy of Chet Baker's vocalisations on Almost Blue reveals how a feminised voice can exist within a masculine housing. Illustrating how this projects animus/anima and, when coupled with an idiosyncratic inflection and timbre it rubs against the viewer-listener to reinforce feelings of loss during Bruce Weber's documentary.

In their respective contributions the theme of masculinity is also widely explored by Phil Powrie and Ian Inglis. In this context Inglis deconstructs the multi-functions of Can't Take My Eyes Off You *from* The Deer Hunter. *His investigations reveal the song as a core element to the film, simultaneously exposing: ritual cohesion; misogyny; sublimated homosexuality; and providing a 'binary opposite' to the Vietnam war scenes that follow. An actual ear, the ear as an unofficial logo for the importance of film sound, (think* Blue Velvet *and* Reservoir Dogs) *once severed, becomes an abject, anal symbol in Powrie's powerful dissection of that latter films famously violent scene. Here, Stealers Wheel's* Stuck In The Middle With You *is shown to be not merely an ironic Tarantinoesque play but a whole set of hidden commentaries on the scenes psychological layers.*

When this book was being compiled the authors were deliberately restricted in several ways. The instructions began with the exclusion of musicals, (as previously discussed) and secondly writers were asked to confine their film selections to the last thirty years, in order to remain 'contemporary', (though there was no such restriction on the songs, providing they were relatively well-known). The final and major limitation imposed was to largely confine their investigations to one song. An invitation list for this experiment was the next phase.

If we are to propose a 'science' of analysing the use of the pop song in contemporary cinema (a branch of the wider science of Image/Text/Sound Studies) then its vanguard of researchers would necessarily have to come from a diverse range of disciplines: audio-visual designers, sound artists, film-theorists, sociologists, composers, marketing experts, curators and poets - as those we have brought together in this book. So as well as providing new insights about audio-visual construction it is hoped that limiting the area of analysis will expose the differences/similarities between contrasting fields of study (and their ways of thinking) in a unique manner. Hirschman and Holbrook are both examples of academics that have extended their fields of study to a point of almost becoming other disciplines. Hirchman's on-going dissection of the film market as a realm of mythology, becomes a form of interpretive marketing so close to media studies that the differences sometimes cease to exist. Here she discusses the myth of Southern USA, as told in the Coen brother's O Brother Where Art Thou, *and how* I Am a Man Of Constant Sorrow, *contributes to a generic mythologised reading for that location.*

[13]

In another guise the popular song is often subjectively associated with a particular time and place, owing to its commercial currency on radio during a specific period. Two people hearing the same song in two different locations doing different things could never draw the same affective associations, on re-hearing, especially if the first time you made love was to that song. If we re-appropriate Roland Barthes' famous terms for the study of the photograph (Camera Lucida) and apply them to the pop-song - we can claim that each song has generalised effect(s) or 'studium' and specific or personal effect(s) activated by each individual beholder 'a punctum' - a little needle-prick of meaning that activates the subjective beyond its general effect. Robynn Stillwell builds on this notion for her essay Clean Reading *discussing a song whose placement can be constantly redefined through its new associations, and how for a single film, a songs intertextual meaning may be entirely different from one year to the next.*

In this regard Tarantino's expressed desire, in Celluloid Jukebox, *that a song belongs to a movie and should never be used for another, is the impossible idea of the purist. Popular tunes appear in TV programmes, during commercials, as parodies or are re-worked by new recording artists, accompanying new video treatments, all dragging their hinterlands of association with them.*

Adorno's patronising warnings about pop, that began our introduction, and which refer not to himself but to a weak willed underclass, boarder on the Nietzschian. The concept of the pop song as a virginal blank, before its cinematic debut, as in Tarantino's perception (hence his general tendency to compile with pre-video era music), is equally flawed. During Like a Virgin Madonna *mocks her received status (amusingly deconstructed in* Reservoir Dogs), *but for song placement, this 'unblemished' stage of development never existed. Songs are defined and redefined from the first time they are heard, and in cinema, the roles like the readings are limitless.*

References

[14]

Adorno, T., & Eisler, H.((1947)1994). *Composing for the Films.* London: Athlone.

Adorno, T. ((1962)1976), *Introduction to the Sociology of Music.* Continuum.

Barthes, R. (1982). *Camera Lucida: reflections on photography.* London: Flamingo.

Chion, M. (1994), *Audio-vision: sound on screen.* Columbia University Press.

Frith, S., Goodwin A., & Grossberg L. (1993), *Sound and Vision: the music video reader.* Routledge.

Gorbman, C. (1987) *Unheard Melodies: narrative film music.* BFI.

Holbrook, M. B. (1993), *The Semiotics of Consumption: interpreting symbolic consumer behavior.* Berlin; New York: Mouton de Gruyter,.

Kassabian, A. (2001) *Hearing Film - Tracking Identifications in Contemporary Hollywood Film Music.* New York, USA: Routledge.

Mulvey, Laura ((1975)1992): '*Visual Pleasure and Narrative Cinema*'. In Caughie et al. (Eds.), op. cit., pp. 22-34. Also published in: Mulvey (1989); Mast et al. (Eds.) (1992), op. cit., pp. 746-57; abridged version in Bennett et al. (Eds.) (1981), op. cit., pp. 206-15; originally published in *Screen* 16(3): 6-18.

Romney, J. (1995), *Celluloid Jukebox Popular Music and the Movies Since the 50s.* London: BFI.

Silverman, K. (1998) *The Acoustic Mirror: The Female Voice in Psychoanalysis and Cinema.* Bloomington: Indiana UP.

Smith, J. (1998), *Sounds of Commerce - Marketing Popular Film Music.* Columbia University Press, pp. 219-220.

Garibaldi Fought Here Dave Beech

I'm Your Man [Leonard Cohen, 1988] / Dear Diary [Nanni Moretti, 1993]

Garibaldi Fought Here

Dave Beech

Leonard Cohen's masochistic love song I'm Your Man *slips into Nanni Moretti's movie* Dear Diary *(1994) as part of a low-profile campaign, like a single flower following a small gift in a chain of seduction. Moretti's film introduces itself without fanfare and razzmatazz - it doesn't hit us between the eyes - but, instead, goes out of its way to extend its welcome.*

Hank Williams' radio show was introduced by a continuity announcer with the simple phrase, delivered with the voice of a market trader, 'howdy neighbours!' Hank built his career on popular sentiment - it served as an anchor and foil for his excess. Music industry professionals tried to steer Hank upmarket[1]. His success was plain to see but the industry couldn't understand it, so didn't trust it to continue. His band members complained that playing his simple tunes would ruin their reputation as musicians[2]. Three-chord hillbilly music had no right to compete with western swing, but Hank Williams trusted his instincts and trusted his audience. 'Play it vanilla' he would tell his band before going on stage and there would be hell to pay if anyone over-elaborated or showed-off. 'Play it vanilla' had, perhaps, a racial connotation[3] to it, but it was technically an instruction to the musicians that the songs were to be played 'plain' because they were not performing for their own pleasure or taste, but that of the audience. Hank Williams's performances were acts of hospitality and his songs were a form of greeting. Every line and every chord said 'howdy', as they welcomed the audience on its own terms and in its own voice.

As a corny welcome, 'howdy neighbours!' is a prime example of what Adorno criticised as the fraudulent happiness and premature reconciliation peddled by mass culture: 'the hostility inherent in the principle of entertainment' (Adorno and Horkheimer 1973 p 136). Its warmth and familiarity compensate for and are contradicted by the calculation and distance required by radio stations/programmes/stars to survive in a competitive market. Greetings, then, can be graded (hostility at one end, hospitality at the other) but it is only the tip of Adorno's iceberg. A particular greeting's full social significance extends beyond, and cannot be read off directly from, its warmth or coldness. A game show host's professional familiarity, for instance, is an act of warmth that is a symptom of the systemic coldness of the culture industry: the industrialisation of welcome is the abolition of warmth in the guise of the smiling face. Adorno's aesthetic thinking, therefore, campaigns for an inverted economy of the greeting, tracing the most aggressive social forces within the most hospitable and popular culture while discovering hope in the most austere and hostile art. As such, Adorno's inverted economy is a valuable corrective to one-dimensional cultural criticism; it cannot, however, be used as a formula for analysing the social life of culture's greeting. If social hope or despair cannot be read off mechanically from a greeting's warmth or coldness, it makes no sense simply to invert the mechanism. Adorno may be a spellbinding advocate for inhospitality in art but we need to guard against taking his analysis as a new equation of inhospitality and hope. Perhaps Adorno makes this mistake himself now and then, overstating the case for cultural austerity or tying hope and inhospitality together too tightly. The essential thing is not to take sides with one style of greeting or another but to examine critically the complex totality of forces brought to bear with each cultural encounter. Cultural forms of attention (in their full social depth)[4] and culture's modes of address (beyond the vagaries of hospitality and hostility) are the basis of the performative deployment of social relations in culture.

What does it mean to engage critically with the social relations that are deployed in a corny welcome or a vangardist affront? In part, it means attending to how culture greets us, rather than reducing cultural engagement to the binary logic of high and low, or the illogic of pluralism, post-modernist or otherwise[5]. Consider, for instance, a film's opening credits. Credit sequences are the first welcome of movies. Fredric Jameson's famous analysis of the opening credits to Star Wars (Jameson, 1983) - that it signals the futuristic tale, in fact, to be a 'nostalgia film' - describes how the film frames itself semiotically for the cinema-going audience. In considering issues around culture's forms of greeting, on the other hand, I am concerned less about how culture frames itself than how culture constructs itself and its audiences through its modes of address. Credit sequences undoubtedly frame the movies they precede, but they also establish the movie's greeting. Star Wars greets us warmly, we might say, insofar as it introduces itself and addresses us in the guise of an anachronistic genre. As such, Star Wars contrives to say 'howdy' even as it prefaces its adventures with an arcane and alien back-story. In place of 'howdy neighbours' Star Wars greets us with something like 'howdy B-movie fans'. In the words of Jameson, it 'satisfies a deep (might I even say repressed?) longing to experience them again' (Jameson 1983). The guise is, indeed, a semiotic matter, as Jameson describes it, but its social effect is carried in its mode of address - and, pace Adorno, its apparent warmth cannot be taken at face value. It's not that a chummy credit sequence is bound to be a disguise for an iron fist or an accountant's calculation. Each howdy welcomes you differently and consequently (to put it moderately) welcomes a different version of you. The radical formulation goes like this: the welcome constructs whoever is welcomed by it; a credit sequence never merely says 'hello', it determines (by singling out and actively forming them) to whom it says 'hello'. It puts us in the correct frame of mind; gets us in the mood; and, prepares us for what is about to unfold. In this way, the performative 'howdy' always places conditions on the welcome and the welcomed.

No soundtrack accompanies Moretti's opening credits to Dear Diary; nor are the credits superimposed on an establishing sequence: they consist of nothing other than names (of the actors) or names and jobs (of the crew). So far, so conventional, perhaps, except that there is a rare tenderness about Moretti's handling of the conventions. Having nothing else to look at or listen to, the longer the credit sequence goes on, the more the viewer is made aware of the value of these individuals. No distractions take our attention away from them as their names are introduced to us one by one (or two by two, in some cases, as they are introduced to us in pairs, like couples). The names are not rushed through at top speed (which always gives the effect that the 'introduction' is merely a legal requirement); each one is given plenty of screen time so that their name can be read at a leisurely pace before passing on to the next one (which gives the impression that they are valued). Would it be too far-fetched to say the pace and the consideration are closer to the introductions a host might make at a dinner party, rather than the acknowledgements made in the culture industry? The resemblance to dinner party introductions is enhanced by the fact that the credits are hand written - the product of a single person's labour, our host. The effect is underlined, and the host identified, in the very first moment of the film proper, when Moretti writes a new page of his diary in the same hand.

What sort of welcome is this? If we are inclined to think of its intimacy as warm and hospitable, its lack of sound and visual spectacle means its hospitality falls some way short of the typical showbiz greeting: entertainment as welcome-on-a-plate, so to speak. There is a certain warmth in the spectacle - a gift of colours, action and music on a grand scale (the bigger the scale, the bigger the welcome, perhaps) - that is entirely lacking in Dear Diary's opening credits. This film addresses us, instead, with a warmth that doesn't exaggerate itself for the sake of impact. Neither does it bypass introductions by winning us over in an instant.

[18]

If the opening credits and the first scene are unspectacular, quiet, humble affairs, then the first sight of the film's star is correspondingly anonymous: Moretti is seen from behind, riding his scooter through the empty, afternoon streets of Rome. One introduction follows another. It is as if Moretti is greeting us tentatively and in stages. He is taking care. It is a slow start compared to the attention seeking standards of the entertainment industry. And the contrast is highlighted by Moretti's voiceover that begins with a lament: 'Summer in Rome, cinemas are closed. All you can see is Sex, Love and Shepherding, Snow White and the Seven Blacks or horror like Henry: Portrait of a Serial Killer or Italian films'. Porn, ultraviolence and a cynical brand of Italian cinema are the targets of a short but pointed complaint by Moretti as we watch him scoot around his favourite streets, showing us not the official Rome of tourism and commerce but his Rome. Following him, we see street after street of a quiet residential Rome, a kind of secret garden in the style of a string of suburban districts. Geography, then, comes to conspire with filmic style and narrated argument to greet us (and thereby configure us) as Moretti's personal guests. Moretti introduces himself to us without any plot to speak of, without spectacle or even a face and, in the same movement, converts us from the mass of strangers that constitutes a cinema audience into new friends, confidantes, intimates.

Moretti scoots on in his element as we hear the boil-in-the-bag philosophising of his well-off but disappointed peers from Italian cinema: 'I'm afraid to re-think my life. I'm a coward. What happened?' When we cut to the scene in which these words are uttered, we are witnesses to a sort of well-heeled penthouse wake in the shape of a small group of professionals moaning into their wine. Stylish interiors and tailored clothes don't compensate for their mawkish sense of subjective impoverishment. 'What has our generation become?' asks one, 'We all changed for the worse. Sold out, compromised, co-opted.' Cut to Moretti sat in the cinema, on edge listening to this self-indulgent mush, saying, 'Why 'all'? This fixation with us 'all' being sold out and co-opted!' Moretti is resisting the cold embrace of his own generation's representatives on the screen in one of the two classic formulations of political struggle[6], one being to represent the experience of the downtrodden as universal, the other (Moretti's) is to call into question the universality of the experience of those in power. Moretti does not identify himself in the role that the movie assigns him and responds wonderfully when the voice of the Italian movie continues, 'We're old, bitter, dishonest. We used to shout awful, violent slogans. Look how ugly we've gotten!' Moretti, now back on his vespa, replies, 'You shouted awful, violent slogans. You've gotten ugly. I shouted the right slogans and I'm a splendid forty-year-old.' Cue Leonard Cohen's song, I'm Your Man.

Later on, Henry, Portrait of a Serial Killer comes to stand for another kind of film Moretti does not want to make - or sit through. Henry is not your man; he is a law unto himself: an ego on the loose. As Moretti makes a few light points against its ultraviolence, He intercuts a few murderous scenes, in which a tubby victim has a television set smashed over his head and another is shot dead while his murderer giggles. If Moretti had objected to violence in a prudish way then these scenes would not appear in his film. Dear Diary is not in denial about violence in the movies and violence in the world. His dispute with the ultraviolent movie does not take the style of the censor or lobbyists of censors, who would stand between the audience and such material, protecting us from it. Moretti includes scenes from an ultraviolent movie in a movie that opposes ultraviolence because he is, above all, interested in establishing a different relationship with the audience, one that is primarily based on mutuality and dialogue. He has introduced himself to us through a string of commitments, beliefs and positions that he holds: he greets us not as a movie star but as a person with an identity, a personality, a history and a geography. And in so doing, Moretti imagines us, the audience, as a group of people who are interested in other people's identities, personalities, histories and geographies because we have them too. Reciprocity is built into Dear Diary by constructing a different sort of relationship between the filmmaker and the audience, by constructing a welcome that is not merely an invitation to pay your money to witness a spectacle. Indiscriminate violence has a knack of catching your attention in the movies - gun shots, bomb blasts, fist fights, bloody bodies and explosions are the pyrotechnics of a movie industry frightened that the audience will be bored if it is not fed a constant diet of bite-size 'events'. Moretti's film is not a firework display at which we gawp and gasp; it does not content itself with merely holding our attention with whatever it takes. Dear Diary is a different kind of film that consequently allows us to be a different kind of audience. What's more, this is as true for fans of ultraviolent movies as anyone else. Moretti walks out of

[19]

the cinema visibly upset as he leaves Henry behind and asks, 'who said good things about this film?' He copies into his diary, word for word, an intellectual defence of the film, as if he is documenting a strange life form. Then he searches out the reviewer (a fantasy scene?) and reads passages back to him. The reviewer curls up, weeping in remorse but Moretti carries on, reading more passages in disbelief and anger. In this way Moretti once again puts dialogue where there once was spectacle, revealing also an emotional inner life at variance with the slick, cynical face of ultraviolence. One of Moretti's greetings, then, could be phrased as, 'howdy ultraviolent fans, here's someone else you are!'

Sat in the cinema, complaining about his peers... this is the first time we see Moretti's face in the film (the next stage in this dialectic of introduction) and he casts himself in the role of the ordinary moviegoer, a viewer talking back to a screen. Moretti's face is revealed, then, at a moment when the actor-director is also a viewer: he is not perceptively different from us. However, this cinemagoer on the screen is not just watching a movie and commenting on it (i.e. watching a movie and resisting its form of address; reconstituting the movie with alternative forms of attention); Moretti is also calling for another kind of movie and is in the process of making such a movie. Before any storyline is in place, Moretti sets up a dialogue about what kind of movie he does and does not want to watch or produce. In contrast to mainstream cinema and TV, which is driven by a star system that commodifies individual identity, Moretti identifies himself in Dear Diary *- shows his face - at the very point at which he wants to distinguish himself, and his sort of movie, from Italian cinema, and also from the comfortable self-loathing of his generation's conservative opinion formers. His identity, therefore, is not reduced to a face; on the contrary, his face becomes the sign of his beliefs, his opinions, his position. He resumes his scooter ride after leaving the cinema again with the back of his helmeted head to the camera. And Leonard Cohen continues to plead his own devotional case: I'm your man.*

[20]

'What I like most is to see houses, neighbourhoods,' Moretti says, 'My favourite neighbourhood is the Grabatella. I wander through the old housing projects. I don't like to see only the facades, I like to see the inside too.' He turns off the road into a courtyard and walks into the building with his scooter helmet still on. In order to gain access to the properties Moretti has to introduce himself in a mask, as Cohen puts it in I'm Your Man, *so that the occupants will accept him. 'I ring the buzzer and pretend I'm location scouting for a film. The tenant asks me what the film is about. I don't know what to say'. He re-enacts this moment for us, in a piece to camera in which he makes up a pitch that might allow him to enter someone else's house. 'It's a film about a Trotskyist pastry chef in Italy during the 1950s', he pauses for a moment to think and completes the description in English, 'a musical'. He is asking to be welcomed. Hank Williams' continuity announcer speaks as the host, welcoming the virtual neighbourhood to Hank's entertainment; posing as a location scout, Moretti greets the residents as their potential guest, so that when he re-enacts this for the camera it is the audience that is put in the position of the host. Moretti, the*

filmmaker, is showing us how the power of the movies can be used as a passport into people's intimate lives, and, at the same time, using the cinema as a foil for his own, more idiosyncratic, pastime. That last sentence is a description of his greeting to the tenant but read it again, now, as a description of what he does to cinema in Dear Diary.

'One day at a penthouse which seemed more affordable', Moretti says, as we see him and his partner, Silvia, both wearing the same style white scooter helmet, looking up at an historical building, 'we asked the price. $700 a square foot!' With Leonard Cohen's I'm Your Man *still watching over the scene, Moretti protests against what Adorno calls 'the ruling principle of reality, which is the principle that all things can be exchanged for other things'.(Adorno 1984) 'You can't talk square feet,' Moretti complains, 'Via Dandolo is a historic street'. And finally, Moretti tells us, as if to put a cherry on the top of his proposition, 'Garibaldi fought here.' Moretti, Garibaldi and Leonard Cohen seem to be in agreement with Oscar Wilde's famous put-down: a man who knows the price of everything and the value of nothing.* Dear Diary *makes this point over and again, from the host's introductions in the opening credits to the next scene, in which Moretti distances himself from the mechanisms of price and profit altogether.*

Pulling up at a traffic light Moretti eyes a young man in a sports car and dismounts. There is no anger in his voice when he says, 'You know what I was thinking?' The driver listens without joining in. 'A very sad thing', Moretti continues, 'even in a more decent society than this one, I'll only feel at ease with a minority of people'. Economically, Moretti takes his point of departure from the roots of capitalist 'mass' culture, in which the cultural product that appealed to the largest majority made the most of its profit margin. This is not the only formula for making money, but it was central to the development of the culture industry, and of the cinema in particular. The first condition of 'mass' culture, therefore, is that it produces and requires (constructs for itself) a 'mass' out of the individuals and groups who come before it, in order to sell to them. Mass culture is a defunct term because it presupposed an homogenous audience (passive recipients, or dupes, in the notoriously pejorative versions). In terms of the greeting, a culture that welcomes its audience as a mass of people cannot help but be centrifugal, in which the product holds the central position from which everything flows. Under these circumstances, the audience can be brought into the calculations but not regarded as individual, contingent or unpredictable. To side with the minority, on the other hand, is not only to prefer the audience to be sovereign in its own contingency but also for those you address to be beyond your calculations. Capitalism likes to think of its markets as pools of 'demand' that justify its 'supply' but Moretti's preference for the minority goes against economic good sense for the sake of the contingent identities hidden by the averages of market research.

[21]

In effect, the majority (mass audience) only exists as an effect of the possibility of calculating its average responses to certain products. A minority is, by contrast, not subject to these broad calculations. For too long the Left (and post-modernists across the board) have equated minorities with elitism, failing to factor in the power necessary to turn a minority into an elite. The minority, then, is not a concept to be preserved for ruling elites but needs to be extended to groups with a kernel of resistance to cultural calculation. In siding with the minority, Moretti is not being elitist in the usual sense, and he makes this clear by distinguishing his love of the minority from both the capitalist exploitation of the masses and the elitist distinction[7] from the herd: 'Not like those films where a couple fights on a desert island because the filmmaker doesn't believe in people. I believe in people, I just don't believe in the majority of people. I'll always be in tune with a minority'. Moretti puts his commitment to the minority to the test by trying to explain it patiently to a complete stranger. The stranger is a minority of one, who, when faced with Moretti's argument about the value of minorities, does not respond. If you can't calculate the response of a minority in the way you can with a majority, you have to be prepared to miss your mark. When the lights change the driver leaves Moretti behind, but not before wishing him 'good luck'. The meeting is not a total failure, then. Moretti gets back to his scooter and continues on his way.

By this point Cohen's I'm Your Man has faded out. It slipped into the movie when Moretti walked out of a cynical Italian movie and it had gone by the time the sports car driver wished him good luck. If the song is anything to go by - and it is - Moretti is a humble sort of film star. Cohen's song confirms Moretti's subversion of the power of the cinema (as spectacle). We are not his audience; he is our man. 'If you want a boxer', Cohen sings, 'I will step into the ring for you'. Whatever or whoever you want, the song says, I'm your man. I'm Your Man is not a boast, though, it is a plea: it is not the arrogant statement of a man who is everything the beloved wants, it is the masochistic promise of a man who will become whatever the beloved asks. It's masochism is not the popularised conception of masochism or the subcultural one but rather a masochism rooted in Sacher-Masoch's Venus in Furs, in which Severin, the swooning narrator, takes an excessive step beyond merely expressing his love. He asks his Venus, Wanda, to marry him and anticipating her rejection, offers himself as her plaything. Severin is not his own man, as they say. Severin is Wanda's man. 'Be a tyrant, be a despot', Severin says, 'but be mine'. (Sacher-Masoch 1991, p.170) Regardless of whether this is his preference or his taste, Severin expresses it differently. It is his plan-B. Severin chooses to be Wanda's slave rather than being apart from her. And the deal he is striking with her is stated clearly and up front when he says, 'If you cannot be mine entirely and forever (by which he means, be my wife) then I want to be your slave, I want to suffer anything to be able to stay by your side'.(Sacher-Masoch 1991,p170). Note the 'if/then' structure. Severin may or may not derive pleasure from pain or of engaging in sexual role-play as a slave (most readers assume that he does); what he says, though, is that he craves a totalising bond with his beloved over and above his own identity, dignity or power - if not a mutually captivated bond, then an asymmetric master-slave one, but at any cost a bond that is total. His slavery is neither inevitable nor his own choice; his love for Wanda engulfs him to the *extent that he cannot live without her, hence he offers her the choice between being his wife and being his tyrant. 'If you want a partner', Cohen sings, 'take my hand or/ if you want to strike me down in anger/ here I stand/ I'm your man'.*

For the lover, the beloved is everything, and in response, the lover promises to become everything. However, when everything equals anything, anything equals nothing. I'm your man, therefore, does not mean I am everything (as in, I fulfil all your desires) but I am nothing (your desires, not mine, are sovereign). I am nothing precisely because I can be anything (tell me your desires and I will conform to them). 'I'm your man' makes no demands on the beloved and asks for nothing in return. In the contract between Wanda and Sacher-Masoch the disappearance of the 'slave' is spelled out in clear terms: 'You shall renounce your identity completely'; 'You have nothing save me; for you I am everything, your life, your future, your happiness, your unhappiness, your torment, your joy'. (Sacher-Masoch 1991)To love is not to ask for more of the beloved but to wish for them more from you. A better you, perhaps. Or a version of you (a particular construction) that pleases the beloved, so that the beloved's happiness is prized above your own. This is why the lover who says, 'I'm your man' is promising to change but going further than that. He is dreaming of multiplying himself. 'And if you want another kind of lover, I'll wear a mask for you': Cohen volunteers all of these possible men and announces, 'I'm your man'. Cohen is your man because he is your men. Moretti is our man because he multiplies himself, too - each scene articulates another Moretti - rather than reducing himself to a single image, character, trait, role, logo. [23]

There is, perhaps, a masochistic edge to all love. Sacher-Masoch elaborates for the first time and in full detail a subjectivity lit up by devotion, longing, worship and adoration for the beloved. I'm Your Man is not just a masochistic love song, then, but a lover's love song - a song characterised by the lover's love of the beloved. The industry standard love song has no love in it, just the cold calculation of business, which is not masochistic (loving) but sadistic (to repeat, cold and calculating). Likewise, the Big Loud Action Movie is sadistic, not only in its spectacularisation and repetition of cruel acts but also in its cold, hard, mechanical, detached, witty, modus operandi. Moretti's film depends on precisely that which 'Big Loud Action Movies have managed to repress, eliminate or overcome: psychological complexity and the registration of accurate social and historical detail'. (Gross, 2000) Big Loud Action Movies drive out human-scale experience with monumentality while Moretti drives out spectacle, in retaliation, with the little dramas of an idiosyncratic, provincial, inner life. Dear Diary is a film that runs on love.

Beauty, Fame, Work, Time, Death, Economics, Atmosphere, Success, Art, Titles, The Tingle, Underwear Power: these are the headings to chapters four to fifteen of Andy Warhol's From A to B and Back Again. The first three chapters are headed 'Love'. This is somewhat surprising, perhaps, since Warhol is undoubtedly the court artist of business. Warhol's works are structured around the commercial practices of reproducibility, de-skilling, uniformity and celebrity (which is all the above). Love sits uncomfortably amongst such criteria. And yet love survives in Warhol's work. Consider, for instance, his preference for those outtakes in which an extra makes a mistake. Instead of rejecting the outtake, Warhol wants to cherish it, as a separate movie, with a new star, the extra who made a mistake. Love exceeds the formula and when the formula is peeled away, as in an outtake, there is a glimpse of love. 'I really don't care that much about 'Beauties'. What I really like are Talkers. To me, good talkers are beautiful because good talk is what I love' (Warhol, 2000). Moretti could have said that in Dear Diary, but it comes from Warhol. 'We are always being told about desire', Barthes said, 'never about pleasure; desire has an epistemic dignity, pleasure does not'. (Barthes, 1975, p.57) Love lacks epistemic dignity as much as the Sacher-Masoch lacks his own identity under the spell of Wanda. Barthes changed the face of cultural criticism by modelling his theory of literature on that of love. From the point of view of reading, Barthes textuality of desire means reserving a place for the uncodified, the intractable and the eccentric. From the point of view of writing, it means hesitancy, longing, loss. 'The text you write must prove to me that it desires me', he wrote, before concluding immediately, 'This proof exists: it is writing'. (Barthes, 1975, p.6) The Post-modernist's view of our manipulated culture conforms to Peter Halley's explanation: 'The regimentation of human movement, activity and perception accompanies the geometric division of space/time. It is governed by the use of time-keeping devices, the application of standards of normalcy, and the police apparatus. In the factory, human movement is made to conform to rigorous spatial and temporal geometries'. (Halley 1989). Love, enthusiasm, euphoria, frank enjoyment of the playful, exuberance, manipulation, spontaneity and beguilement of the senses seem naïve by comparison, but perhaps less so under Barthes' motto: 'Incoherence seems to me preferable to a distorting order.' (Barthes 1982, p.3).

[24]

Meaning is never monogamous in Barthes' account, nor is writing a comforting exchange with a welcoming reader. Writing is an embrace that has no grip. In this sense, everything that Barthes wrote was a fragment of a lover's discourse: a text written in response to amorous disappointment and rejection. Writing, as an embrace that has no grip, is invitation. A film greets us, also, as a welcome that has no firm control over us. The point of using formula in Hollywood is to compensate for the audience's unpredictability. Dear Diary adds one greeting to another in order to place love and dialogue above the spectacle - it is an invitation to Moretti that stands in for an invitation to a different kind of culture as well as different modes of address and different forms of attention. Warmth is not enough. Accepting an invitation amounts to submitting to its authority and, by doing so, contributing to its authority. This is why Derrida's investigation into the politics of friendship has made its greatest insight by deconstructing the Kantian opposition of hospitality and hostility. Welcoming the stranger as a friend (as a proxy friend, we might say) is a virtue perhaps but it is not without its economy of power. Hospitality moderates the split between friend and stranger without confusing the roles of host and guest. In fact, from a structural point of view, it could be said that the hospitable elision of the friend/stranger opposition preserves the vital distinction between host and guest. Mastery conditions hospitality. If, in Kant, hospitality is owed to the stranger as a duty, it follows that the host receives authority in the very act of welcoming. Hospitality is possible only on the condition that it is impossible. Welcoming the stranger into the economy of the household, of which the host is master, means to submit the stranger to the host's mastery. For there to be hospitality, Derrida says, there must be a door. But if there is a door, and there must be, then hospitality is hostile to the stranger. Someone has a key to the door, Derrida adds, which means that someone controls the conditions of hospitality. Indeed, hospitality is the door - the threshold - that closes onto the world of strangers in order to be able to permit entry to strangers-as-friends.

Hospitality is hostile to the stranger by virtue of demanding the stranger be greeted as a friend. The stranger is not an intruder but a friend when the host authorises the guest as a proxy friend. Hospitality is opposed to hostility - which fixes the stranger-as-stranger - so as to be more effectively hostile to the stranger. It would be a mistake to think of hospitality as hostile only inasmuch as it administers (rations, legislates, selects) passage across the threshold; hospitality is hostile to the guest through the effect of including the stranger in the law of the 'house'. To accept an invitation, therefore, is to codify oneself, or allow oneself to be so codified, and thereby to submit to the 'house rules'. Invitations are not issued without conditions; they are demands for proper behaviour. Effectively, to welcome a stranger as a friend, then, is to convert the stranger into a friend in order to welcome them as a guest. The guest is the iteration of the stranger that submits to the mastery of the host. Only the host has the authority to issue invitations. Hence, every invitation is a coded - in both senses, of cryptic and semiotic - order to comply. And, the warmth of the welcome assures compliance. The friendlier the host, the more efficient is the conversion of the stranger into the guest. That is to say, the ebullient host allows the guest to believe that the authority of the host is not being imposed at all. Likewise, the more inviting the invitation, the more conspicuous is the concealment of the hostility within hospitality.

[25]

Derrida's warning about the hostility concealed within hospitality should not be underestimated. It has a very important contribution to make to our understanding of culture, especially culture's forms of attention and modes of address. Like Adorno's critique of 'mass' culture's fraudulent happiness and premature reconciliation, Derrida unfolds the greeting with devastating effect. Unlike Adorno, though, Derrida does not give any reason for equating cultural hostility with hope. He gives no clear indication of hope at all. For this we need to return to Barthes, I think, for whom hope lies in love and the dialogue of writing's (culture's) address. This is Moretti's hope, also. 'Anything is likely to ravish me which can reach me through a ring, a rip, a rent', Barthes said, 'the first time I saw X through a car window: the window shifted, like a lens searching out who to love in the crowd; and then - immobilized in some accuracy of my desire? - I focused on that apparition whom I was henceforth to follow for months' (Barthes 1990). To be ravished by the *fragment, fascinated by the occluded scene and immobilized by the chance encounter is, in Barthes, to prefer care to justice and prize parochial sentiment over universal truth. In the 80s, cultural theory coerced artists into getting things right; Barthes gives us higher ambitions. Even amidst the technical orrery of* Myth Today, *Barthes chose to clarify the relationship between signifier and signified with the example of a bunch of roses given to a lover. Philosophers have typically preferred to talk about tables and other dull objects in order to foreground the analysis at hand; Barthes illustrates the liveliness of signs by talking about 'passionified' roses. Instead of the 'pious show' of standard critique and academic achievement, Barthes closes in on the world and its passions. Semiological theory was never Barthes' attempt to absolve the intellectual from the everyday, the contingent and emotional life. On the contrary, it places the writer among the manure of contradictions in which the writer is always implicated by writing. The theory of signs does not indulge itself in a show trial in which the culture industry (or some other false rival) is tried for crimes against culture and found perpetually guilty. When he writes 'Take a bunch of roses: I use them to signify my passion' (Barthes 1982), it is Barthes himself who is offering the roses, and, perhaps, it is the reader directly who is being asked to take them.*

Do we project charm onto Moretti - in the absence of character, action, plot - and see him, magically, as 'our man', the man we want him to be at this early stage of the movie? When the film has hardly begun, and perhaps only because the film has hardly begun, the actor-director is all the men we want. Moretti uses the exploratory early part of the film, when nothing has settled, as a space in which he can multiply himself and thereby establish a relationship with the moviegoer that is not based on the spectacle. This is a Barthesian greeting. Moretti multiplies himself and refuses to reduce himself to an image as he introduces himself to us. But: although he is the multiplied lover who introduces himself to us over and again, is it not us, the multiple, anonymous audience who is being cast as his lover? He multiplies himself for a beloved that is already, literally multiple: us. Moretti scoots along on his vespa to the sound of Cohen singing I'm Your Man *and Moretti is our man. At the same time, though, the song is clearly extra-diegetic: Moretti doesn't sing it and there is no indication that he has heard it. The song is for us. Perhaps we associate the song with him and attribute it to him, but it is us that listen to it. Cohen's song is for us, and we are induced into singing it for Moretti. Sat in the cinema, tapping our feet, following the beat with a finger or slapping the arm of the chair, it is the audience who is chiming with Cohen, whispering the words or following them in our heads: 'I'm your man'. You might not necessarily feel utterly devoted to the author a la Sacher-Masoch, but you have at least devoted your time, your attentiveness, something of yourself. After all, isn't that what attending to someone else's movie, essay, artwork or song is like?*

[26]

Notes

1 *Fred Rose, a country music producer and songwriter who worked with the leading performers of his day, including Roy Acuff and Hank Williams, wrote a letter to Billboard magazine in 1946 com-*

plaining about industry put-downs of country music. 'We call it 'hillbilly' music and sometimes we're ashamed to call it music', he said. Interestingly, Rose himself came from a Jazz background and converted to country after hearing Roy Acuff. Hank, in 1952, said, 'Fred Rose came to Nashville to laugh'. He knew about the pressure to take country music upmarket because he'd been on the other side.

2 'If you played with Hank', R. D. Norred, his steel guitarist, once said, 'you was kinda looked down on'.

3 It's possible to imagine 'play it vanilla' as an instruction to keep the music white, meaning hillbilly rather than Jazz or Blues. However, Hank went on record saying 'all the music training I ever had was from [Rufus Payne]'. Payne was a black street musician who taught Hank the importance of rhythm, and is sometimes credited with the blues flavour that distinguished Hank from his country peers at the time.

4 For a discussion of the critical approach to cultural forms of attention, see the theoretical debate around 'philistinism' in Beech & Roberts et al., The Philistine Controversy, London: Verso, 2002.

5 For a discussion of pluralism see my review of Arthur Danto's 'The Wake of Art' in Historical Materialism, Volume 10, Issue 2, pp. 255-266.

6 See Ernesto Laclau, Emancipation(s), Verso, 1996 and Butler, Laclau, Zizek, Contingency, Hegemony, Universality, Verso, 2000.

[27]

7 Distinction, in cultural matters, is not a neutral term that connotes difference alone. Bourdieu has shown that cultural division is structured by the operations of distinction through cultural capital.

References

Adorno,T. Horkheimer, (1973) *The Dialectic Of Enlightenment*, Verso.

Barthes (1975) *The Pleasure of the Text*, Basil Blackwell.

Barthes, R. (1990) *A Lover's Discourse*, London, Penguin. p192.

Barthes, R. (1982). *Selected Writings*, Oxford University Press. p97.

Gross, L (2000) *Big And Loud. Action/Spectacle/Cinema; a sight and sound reader*, BF1. pp3-8.

Halley, P. Jameson, F. (1983) *Postmodernism and Consumer Society*, in Foster, H (ed) *Postmodern Culture*, Pluto Press. p116.

Sacher-Masoch, L. (1991) 'Venus in Furs', in G. Deleuze and L. Sacher-Masoch *Masochism*. New York: Zone Books trans. Jean McNeil.

Warhol, A. (1975) *From A to B And Back again: the Philosophy Of Andy Warhol*, Picador.

Heavy Rotation *Matthew Caley*

The End [The Doors, 1967] / Apocalypse Now, Redux [Ford-Coppola, 1979/2001]

Heavy Rotation

Matthew Caley

Apocalypse Now *is a heavy film. This quality of heaviness lies not only in its subject-matter, its stars, its director's ambition, its reputation, in the epic, logistical effort of its making, or even its underlying themes - it lies also in the web of literary allusions that weave themselves through the narrative. Scriptwriter John Milius not only used Joseph Conrad's novella* Heart Of Darkness *as the loose template for the film, he also managed to employ T. S Eliot's poems* The Hollow Men *(whose initial-planned epigraph from Corad 'The horror, the horror' became the film's famous coda) and particularly* The Wasteland *- together with the anthropological, mythic works such as Jessie L Weston's* From Ritual To Romance *and J. G Frazer's* The Golden Bough *which Eliot cited as influences on his grand opus. These books in turn brought in the story of* The Fisher King *and the legend of* The Holy Grail *- stories of mythic quest which relate to Willard's own. As* The Wasteland *itself is a modernist collage of allusions - to Dante, Chaucer, Shakespeare, Wagner, Baudelaire, Spencer, Ovid, Homer, Herman Hesse amongst others - these references also lodge themselves into the film's already overcrowded mythology. According to Milius:*

> 'Willard is Adam, Faust, Dante, Aeneas, Hickleberry Finn, Jesus Christ, the Ancient Mariner, capt. Ahab, Odysseus, and Oedipus'.

> *(Richard Thompson, 'Stoked: An Interview With John Milius'* Film Comment *12, July/August 1976, p. 15).*

The problem with such literary portentiousness is that it becomes a heavy burden for any film to bear and is certainly not warranted as structural necessity - it exists as an unearnt layering, possibly useful for the scriptwriter, less so for the beholder/reader of the film. I'd like to argue in this essay that real poetic structures - the inter-relation of image/text/sound - exist in this film and add a saving 'lightness' to the heaviness of its construction. I want to do this through an examination of the opening sequence of Apocalypse Now *- looking closely at the use of* The Door's *song* The End *over Willard's dervish dance under the ceiling-fan.*

Whenever the word 'poetic' is applied to a film we usually have good reason to worry. The casual misappropriation of this vague formulation usually signals the visual dreamscapes, sublime pastorals, and exotic juxtapositions of the worst kind of heavy 'arthouse' movie. Poetic theory itself long ago shed every vestige of this neo-Romantic woolliness - urged as early as 1910 by Ezra Pound to sheer itself of heavy Georgian decoration, to ply clarity of perception/image - the thing presented - against clarity of perception/image. Pound - an exiled American drawn to Eastern thought - was attracted to the Chinese ideogram, the way in which three separate images form themselves into a separate concept. The ideogram was attractive to Pound because he realised that a poem was a construct in which the image/text/sound inter-relation was inherently embedded, enabling him to dispense with traditional structures of rhythm and rhyme in favour of 'rhyming' actualities. The structure of his magnum opus The Cantos *eschewed rhyme in favour of 'rhyming' actualities and ideas - in the manner of the ideogram - ideas and actualities such as different religious beliefs, of heaven or the afterlife, hell, economic theories in relation to war, the selling of munitions, usura, and particularly the rise and collapse of empires from different time-zones - real and mythical - within history. Other modernist poets followed his lead in developing this harder structural approach to the poetic: William Carlos Williams famously describing the poem as a machine made of words. Consider this poetic fragment by Pound-disciple Jonathon Williams:*

air in a hornet's nest

over the water makes a

solid, six-sided music

Guy Davenport, in his essay on Williams says:

Any poem worth its salt is as transparently complex as (this) wherein every quality is mirrored in another (and an aria and a horn are camouflaged into the richness); that the lines are typo-graphically isometric, seven-syllabled, and inwardly ornamental (-net's nest, solid/sided; s, m and n so placed as to make a bass line to the treble) is as native an instinct to the poet as the hornet's hexagonal architecture.

[31]

(Davenport, p. 184).

(We might consider Williams' poetic fragment in relation to the famous sequence in Apocalypse Now: *Air Cavalry's dawn helicopter raid on the Viet Cong village accompanied by Richard Wagner's* Ride Of The Valkyries *or read it over a recording of Stockhausen's* Helicopter Quartet*).*

This is truly 'poetic' machinery at work: image/text/sound interlocked and interchangeable, a hard clarity of perception delivered with lightness.

A film - like most cultural production - adverts, multi-media, much graphic design, much contemporary arts practice - is also a construct made up of image/text/sound. Within a film these elements form a triangle of inter-relation but not one where each element of the triangle can be separately delineated from each other - they merge, overlap, leak into each other. However, to get a basic purchase on the three elements of the triangle within the total field of the film we can begin to delineate them thus:

Image
Filmic 'shot' or sequence of shots/stills.
Specific objects/images within the above.

Text
Film-script, dialogue/'original' source text or book
sub-titles/inter-titles/song-lyrics,
heard or inferred.

Sound
Diegetic, non-diegetic sound:
music, natural or substituted sound.

Within the opening sequence of Apocalypse Now - we might construct a basic triangle/ideogram thus:

[32]

> **Image**
> *Ceiling-fan*
> *(Jim Morrison's/The Door's image).*

Text
The Door's song 'The End'.

Sound
The whirr of the helicopter blades.

The 'form-edit' between the ceiling-fan in Willard's Saigon hotel-room and the helicopter blades has become one of the most visible/audible hallmarks of Walter Murch's brilliant sound-editing throughout the film, but less has been said about the triangular relationship between these two elements and the aural/textual construct of the song The End. *Here, the triangle of image/text/sound asserts itself into a field of meanings far more akin to the 'ideogram' of Pound's poetic theory than any spurious notion of 'poetic' film or any weighty layering of literary allusion.*

Obviously, the Coppolla/Murch conceit of having The End *at the beginning - as an misplaced 'aural End credit' reverses film narrative - or puts the narrative in a potential nightmarish, eternally-returning loop. The Nung/Congo river becomes an ox-bow lake which in turn re-employs the already fruitful ceiling-fan/helicopter blade composite image as an unempathetic symbol of* the film-projector. 'All films proceed in the form of an indifferent and automatic unwinding, that of the projection, which on the screen and through the loudspeakers produces simulacra of movement and life - and this unwinding must hide itself and be forgotten' (Chion, p. 9). Both this war and the revolution against it were televised - a point emphasised by Coppolla and film crew's later Hitchcock - (as self-displaying-auteur) - like cameo later on in the beach-landing scene.

It should be noted here that Jim Morrison as poet is no poet at all - his poems as poems are 6th Form mysticism and his song-lyrics taken by themselves are infected by the very same literary portentiousness that burdens the movie. But Morrison/The Doors as songwriters/collaborators providing image/text/sound to this opening scene are much closer to the poetic model outlined above - the proper interplay between image/text/sound within the song (its hinterland of connotation) and its further interrelation with the film.

Crucial here is the dark 'hidden' pun on the word 'revolution' created by that interrelation, both as in 'complete rotation'/'going around in circles' and 'the overthrow of the established order' which themselves represent how history does indeed tend to repeat itself - revolutions overthrow the established order then become the established order and need themselves to be overthrown. At the macro-level Jim Morrison and The Doors stand here as representatives of the entire counter-culture's revolution against the Vietnam War and at the micro-level we have the Willard/Kurtz Oedipal struggle.

[33]

The quality of Jim Morrison's voice harks back to the aural rotundity of Elvis Presley's timbre rather than the more adenoidal vocalisations favoured by the other major rock singers of the period (Dylan, Lennon - singers with arguably greater 'anti-war' credentials and therefore more obvious soundtrack choices than Morrison) - its is both of the belly and bellicose, a rounded yet 'slightly-hoarse tenor baritone' (Hopkins/Sugerman, p. 82) infused with a hint of the crooner. Mirroring Brando's progress (sic) from the hard-muscled blue-collar Kowalski (Streetcar Named Desire) to the brooding, authoritarian hulk of Kurtz, the resonance of that voice, its full-bodied emanation, seems to evoke Morrison's own progress (sic) from rakish 'Lizard King' to the corpulent alcoholic of his final 'end' years - from sinuous potential to the weight of 'legend'.

This vocal quality or grain of voice brings heft and authenticity to those sometimes overly-florid, consciously-dramatic lyrics - poetry as 'the idea of poetry' rather than poetry itself - which despite this do include such exhortations as 'The west is best' and 'All the children are insane' which obviously link thematically to the upheaval of Vietnam. The song also contains an Oedipal scenario, not heard in this opening sequence but with a strong ghost-presence nevertheless. 'Father I want to kill you' pits Willard/Morrison - Willard's filmic beginning thrashing about in an alcoholic stupor in a hotel room in Saigon, Morrison going to his end in a drug-induced stupor in a rented apartment in Paris. They are wayward sons to the dark and heavy father(s) of American *patriarchy - the obese slob at the end of the river, the minotaur at the centre of the maze. Thus the film's beginning continues to prefigure and enclose its end - the sacrificial slaying of the cow a kind of parody of fertility rites - the withering of the crop of American youth.*

(In this context we can also ponder on Morrison's other military-metaphor-song The Unknown Soldier *being premoniscent of his own demise - the body never found, the symbolic headstone in Pere Lachaise - a dissoluted and then fully disappeared body fleshing out his own myth and further emphasising the missing generation of American youth.)*

Played at the film's beginning, The End, *rotates the ceiling-fan/helicopter-blades/radial palm/film projector, fast forwarding us to the 'end' of the film - 'weird scenes inside the goldmine' to Kurtz' cave - where Conrad's vision of a near-anorexic Kurtz:*

> I saw the thin arm extended... his body (   ) pitiable and appalling the cage of his ribs astir,
> the bones of his arms waving..

> *(Conrad)*

has thickened into a true film 'heavy' - Brando swollen to 250lbs.

[34]

> 'Father ...I want to kill you'.

The 'heavy', druggy, lysergic atmosphere of the song together with Morrison's druggy image form a powerful corollary to the experience of many soldiers in Vietnam - seeing this first 'rock 'n' roll war' as like some Bosch hallucination, they took drugs to further the sense of the burden of unreality or escape from it, lighten it.
LANCE: Hey, you know that last tab of acid I was saving?
CHEF: Yeah
LANCE: I dropped it.
CHEF: You dropped acid. Far out.
Drug intake, particularly LSD intake, can play havoc with the subject's experience and measurement of time. Jim Morrison took the name of The Doors from Aldous Huxley's famous account of the drug-experience The Doors Of Perception. *Huxley notes of taking 'peyote':*

> (that) along with indifference to space there went an even more complete indifference to time.
> My actual experience had been, was still, of an indefinite duration or alternatively of a perpet-
> ual present made up of one continually changing apocalypse.

> *(Huxley)*

Yet again we find ourselves in a loop of eternal occurrence, the record stuck in its groove. 'There were heartbeats from Ray's organ, sudden ejaculations from John's drums, sitar-like excursions from Robby's guitar'. (Hopkins/Sugerman, 1980). The musical nuances of the song itself encompass a West/East dialectic - the Western rock foundation of drums and base vying for our attention with the distinctly Eastern guitar figures that drift across the song's structure like the drifts of smoke across the jungle-palms, whose exotic radials re-emphasise the helicopter/ceiling fan motif.

In his essay The Corporeality of the Filmic Discourse *an exploration of the body in film, Patrick Fuery shows how the body can be made to signify ideological function, citing the particular framing of Bruce Willis' body in* Die Hard *(McTeirnan, 1988):*

> It is the Americanised body - that of the supposed normal (American) man against the foreign bodies (the viral?) of the Ubermensch.

(Fuery, p. 76)

Willard's filmic body and Morrison's (dis)embodied/voice 'duet' in these opening scenes as representatives of the youthful body in distress - Oedipalised by society and The Law Of The Father - to destroy that which created them. In this sense, Willard/Morrison is both son to Kurtz - as is indicated by the upside-down crops of his head as he lies on the hotel bed which prefigure Kurtz/Brando's head iconically framed by light and shadow as he lies in his cave at the film's end - but will eventually become/replace him by killing him - a kind of Abraham/Isaac inversion. Fuery helps us here by linking the spectacle of the body to the body of the condemned:

[35]

> it is held up not simply as corporeal function, but rather as an identification of the institution of power and force over the body, and at the same time the body's potential to resist and disrupt these structures of power.

(Fuery, p. 82)

Within the dialectics of power explored by Apocalypse Now *Willard/Morrison's body is subject to the full weight of this formulation.*

> Apocalypse Now (Coppola, 1979) relies on the altered body of Brando to physically demonstrate the force of an obsession.

(Fuery, p. 85)

We should return here to the ceiling-fan. So far we have seen the ceiling fan 'rotated' by the eternally-recurring loop of the film, activated by The End *being at the beginning and by the hidden pun of 'revolution', together with merging via 'form-edit' with the whirr of the helicopter's rotating-blades. In addition to this, a history of the ceiling-fan in cinema would reveal it to be a sign of film-noire, of the exotic and of heat. Gilbert Adair firms up these connections in his* Hollywood's Vietnam *book of essays:*

> Willard's hotel room is a mess. Its overflowing ashtrays, empty beer cans and rumpled sheets suggest the squalid, vaguely pornographic clutter of some down-at-heel private detective, a Sam Spade or Philip Marlowe.(Co-incidentally, in Heart Of Darkness the equivalent of Sheen's character is named Marlow.)

(Adair, p. 148)

In this opening sequence the 'film-noire' signifier of the ceiling-fan presides over a collapse of the interior/exterior. Willard is grounded inside the non-space of a hot anonymous hotel room in Saigon, his mind turning over his previous experience of jungle warfare - semi-naked, then naked, he 'goes native' under the sign of the ceiling-fan/helicopter-blade/radial palm-frond - in Mileu/Coppola's grand scheme this is a Dionysian revelry, a purifying of the body before the long quest and a pre-figuring of the climactic sacrifice at the end/beginning of that quest.

The stuffy, claustrophobic, heavy atmosphere is broken for a few brief seconds when Willard approaches the slatted blinds of the window - the actual threshold of inside/outside - and speaks for the first time in the present moment, not as voice-over narrator:

Saigon, shit.

'The End' is temporarily ended here - or postponed - whilst he delivers this alliterative expletive - we glimpse an ordinary street, people going about their daily business - the only such sliver of normality in the entire film. The nightmarish loop is halted to give us a brief glimpse of the world which Willard no longer inhabits, is cut off from. The Doors vanish and a window replaces them - yet we might hear the feint echo of another Morrison song Break On Through *(to the other side) first hinted at in the tentative peak through the blinds then violently over-signalled in his smashing of the mirror with his fist.*

When The End *returns it is with its most disturbed section - Morrison is gulping, grunting, squawking, inarticulate, inchoate, animalistic; the music is swirling, booming, grating. It's as if that single glimpse of normality triggers Willard/Morrison into their frenzied* pas-de-deux, *a sweating out of any last drop of humanity.*

In his essay The Romans In Films *(Mythologies p. 26) Barthes cites sweating in Mankiewicz's* Julius Caesar *(where incidentally the youthful Marlon Brando plays another troubled military commander Mark Anthony) as a sign of interior conflict. The ceiling-fan, the function of which is to cool, here operates semiotically as its opposite - signifying the exotic heat of foreign climes in which the soldier(s) suffer, heating up the room and Willard's interior distress - sweating out the virus within him:*

Lost in a Roman wilderness of pain.

('The End')

The song The End *helps to collapse time by locating us simultaneously in the 1967 Hot Summer Of Love and its proto-revolutionary fervour, and in contemporary time-looking back on this disastrous war with hindsight; the ceiling-fan collapses inside/outside - the hotel room merges with the jungle; Willard's ideological body in distress merges with his inner angst, Willard trashes the hotel room in a classic rock 'n' roll gesture, Jim Morrison 'collapses' on stage during an orgiastic performance, Kurtz collapses in his cave, hacked; naked, Martin Sheen collapses with a heart attack, Jim Morrison collapses in his bath; Willard collapses.*

Coppolla, Brando, Morrison, the Vietnam war, Wagner ('German music is a heavy music' - Kundera), Eliot, Conrad - Apocalypse Now *as a major spectacle both lumbers and soars. The danger here, aside from the already outlined charge of portentiousness, as critics such as Frank P. Tomasulo have pointed out, is that there's a very real chance of the audience becoming:*

[37]

implicated in the exhilarating superiority of the American attack.

(Tomasulo)

that we glorify in the heaviness, the hardware, the pyrotechnics, the scale. Gilbert Adair cites French critic Andre Bazin's idea of 'the Nero complex':

the vicarious pleasure afforded by the representation of large-scale scale destruction.

(Adair, p. 151)

One symptom of the film's impact and dissemination throughout popular culture is the eternal recycling of Kilgore's 'I love the smell of Napalm in the morning' as an enjoyable joke, of a heaviness deflected into lightness. Yet perhaps the argument about whether the film is anti/pro war, whether it glorifies war or not, is not quite sufficient to gauge the complexity of our response.

In his novel The Unbearable Lightness Of Being *(the film of which had Walter Murch as sound-designer) Milan Kundera weaves the themes of 'light' and 'heavy' throughout the text, linking this to Nietzsche's idea of eternal return - positing the example that if the French revolution were to recur eternally, French historians would be less proud of Robespierre but as they are dealing with something that does not return, then the bloody history of the revolution is turned into mere words, theories and discussions, has become lighter than feathers, frightening to no-one. He starts by putting the case negatively by saying that the mad myth of eternal return says that a life which disappears once and for all, which doesn't return, is merely a shadow, without weight, dead in advance, and whether it was horrible, beautiful or sublime, its horror, sublimity and beauty mean nothing. In this terrifying prospect that our lives recur a number a times, the weight of unbearable responsibility lies heavy on every move we make, which is why Nietzche called the idea of eternal return the heaviest of burdens - and if this is true, Kundera continues - then our lives can stand out against it in all their splendid lightness. However, the heavier the burden, the closer our lives come to the earth, the more real and truthful they become and conversely, the absence of burden causes man to be lighter than air, to soar into the heights. Therefore we are caught between the poles of heaviness and lightness, trying to gauge which one is negative, which positive.*

[38]

The Vietnam War has been and gone, but through Apocalypse Now *and other movies of its ilk is in a state of eternal recurrence in our culture-as simulacra, as aftertrace. The hidden pun on 'revolution', born out of the relationship between ceiling-fan, song and helicopter-blades in* Apocalypse Now's *opening sequence invokes the notion of a terrible re-occurrence - the end becoming the beginning, signifying the heaviest of burdens whilst simultaneously, through the very nature of its ideogrammic, triadic set of relations, maintaining a truly poetic structure, an ambiguous but saving lightness.*

References

French, K. (1998)*Apocalypse Now*. 2nd ed., London: Bloomsbury.

Barthes, R. (1972) *Mythologies*. London: Vintage.

Davenport, G. (1984) *The Geography Of The Imagination*. 2nd ed., London: Picador.

Kundera, M. (1984) *The Unbearable Lightness Of Being*.12th ed., London: Faber & Faber.

Chion, M. (1994) *Audio-Vision*. New York: Columbia University Press.

Woodward, A. (1980) *Ezra Pound And The Pisan Cantos*. London: Routledge.

Ditmar, L & Michaud G. (2000) *From Hanoi To Hollywood*. 3rd ed., Rutgers University Press.

Fuery, P. (2000) *New Developments In Film Theory*. MacMillan Press Ltd.

Hopkins, J. & Sugerman, D. (1980) *No One Here Gets Out Alive*. 3rd ed., London: Plexus.

Adair, G. (1981) *Hollywood's Vietnam*. London/New York: Proteus Books.

Huxley, A. *The Doors Of Perception*. London: Flamingo-Harper-Collins.

Conrad, J. *Heart Of Darkness*. England: Penguin.

Two Jews Wander Through The Southland *Elizabeth C. Hirschman*

I Am A Man Of Constant Sorrow [Soggy Bottom Boys, 2000] / O Brother Where Art Thou [Coen Brothers, 2000]

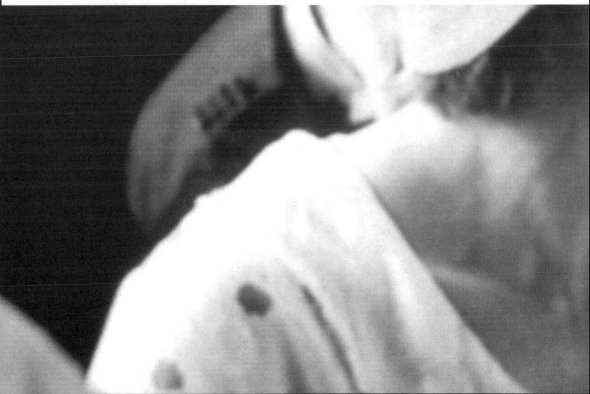

Two Jews Wander Through the Southland

Elizabeth C. Hirschman

The auteur view of filmmaking proposes that the writer, director and other creative personnel contributing to a motion picture project upon it their souls, perceptions, prejudices and world views. From this vantage point, I see the song, Man of Constant Sorrow, *as an allusion to Joel and Ethan Coen's Jewish roots. I also interpret the protagonist of* Oh Brother *(2000), Ulysses Everett McGill as personifying the Coen's ideology in the film. I argue that this results in a negatively stereotyped portrayal at the American Southland - the place where I was born and raised.*

Introduction

The motion picture Oh Brother Where Art Thou *(2000) was written, produced and directed by Joel and Ethan Coen, a collaborative team of brothers who have brought several other notable, off-beat films to the screen over the past two decades[1]. Joel and Ethan are Jewish and although born and raised in Minneapolis, Minnesota, they attended film school in New York City - that hotbed of Judaic artistic and commercial creativity that includes figures such as Allen Ginsberg, Stephen Sondheim, Woody Allen, Carole King, Irving Berlin and Leonard Bernstein. What is interesting about all of the above creators and the Coen brothers, as well, is that despite having an 'ethnic' background, they bring to their work products a seemingly universal poignance and human empathy that crosses most (though not all) ethnic, racial and religious boundaries. The characters created on screen by the Coen brothers follow this same heritage, yet expand it by fixing upon perverse, bizarre and frighteningly genuine activities of human behaviour that simultaneously attract and repel the audience. As in the case of the kidnapping-gone-wrong in* Fargo, *we find ourselves transfixed by disgust, even as we are overcome by curiosity.*

Yet unlike the works by, say, Allen Ginsberg, Woody Allen, or Carole King, which are filled with autobiographical material, the Coen brothers' films have seemed, up to now, to be far removed from their personal lives. The cuckolded husband of Blood Simple, *the child-desperate parents of* Raising Arizona, *the money-desperate car salesman of* Fargo, *all seemed to be created from whole cloth, so to speak; cloth that was woven far away from the Coen's direct experience.*

In Oh Brother, *however, I am going to argue that we glimpse for the first time the Coen's self-images emerging through their creative canvas. They are embodied in the character of Ulysses Everett McGill, played in the film by George Clooney. At the outset of the narrative, the Coen's alert us to their intention to re-tell the Homeric tale of Ulysses - that misdirected wanderer, lost husband and father, tormented soul, and classic, tragic victim of hubris. To orient us thusly, the message 'A wanderer, harried for years on end...' is imprinted on the screen.*

And yet, this claim is unconvincing (to me at least) because although the tale told does mimic Ulysses' journey in analogous details and includes two co-wanderers, DelMar, a hapless farmer, and Pete, a would-be restauranteur, the spirit of the story is not Odysseyan but rather Judaic, and in particular, the trials and tribulations of the biblical Job.

Like Job, Ulysses Everett McGill remains an optimist in the midst of his ongoing misfortunes; these torments, however, we realize are to be never-ending. There is no re-arrival back home where the final enemy is slain and the wife and child happily embrace the father. Rather, in the Coen's version, the tired traveler returns home after his long and arduous journey to a hen-pecking wife and seven similarly-inclined daughters. He may earn a living, but he will never earn their respect and admiration. Although as Ulysses-Everett proclaims, he is the Paterfamilias, he will remain forever the schlemiel.

A Man of Constant Sorrow

This reasoning brings us to the central musical image in the film - the song Man of Constant Sorrow. *This theme performed by the Soggy Bottom Boys and arranged by Carter Stanley on the soundtrack, is the essence of Ulysses Everett McGill's character.*

Although Ulysses is highly intelligent, optimistic, ambitious, pragmatic, verbally gifted and scientifically enlightened, he is and shall forever remain a man of constant sorry:

[43]

I am a man of constant sorrow, I've seen trouble all my days. I bid farewell to old Kentucky, the place where I was born and raised.

In trouble for six long years, no pleasure here on earth I've found. I have no friends to help me down. I'm just a stranger, I'll meet you on God's golden shore.

Now, as is quite evident, this is not the kind of song a genuine Ulysses would be singing. No, Ulysses would be bellowing something along the lines of Freddy Mercury's We are the Champions. *Or as Homer himself would put it:*

Though we are not the strength we were in former years, we shall not cease to strive, to seek, to find, and not to yield...

But because the Coen's Ulysses is Jewish, and not Greek, he, like Job, will wander through obstacle after obstacle, providing witty verbal commentary, fastidious in his personal grooming practices, and ending up precisely where he started - an apologizing husband and father, disrespected by his family yet sill optimistic that his lot in life will somehow improve. After all, as he notes, 'They're bringing electricity to this place; everything's going to be put on a grid, modernized ...'. Surely then, life will be equitable and he will receive his due rewards.

The Southland as Wilderness

The travels and travails through which the Coens' propel their fictitious, yet metaphorically autobiographical, Ulysses are especially revealing projections of their urban, Judaic heritage. I remember seeing the 1976 motion picture by John Boorman, Deliverance (1972), with my New York Jewish husband and a few years later the 1978 film Cool Hand Luke (1967), with him, as well. The South they portrayed seemed to etch itself indelibly on his Hebrew consciousness; and I suspect the same traumatic viewing occurred to the Coen brothers at an impressionable age.

From these two films, one glimpses the geographic vista south of the Mason-Dixon line as a terrifying wilderness filled with rapacious, sodomizing hillbillies, corrupt, fat white politicians, sunglass-clad sheriffs in cowboy hats and armed with shotguns astride horses keeping watch over chain gangs sweltering along rural roadsides mindlessly crushing rocks with fifty-pound sledgehammers, pursuing escaped prisoners with a pack of braying bloodhounds and a lynching rope.

[44]

From Cat on a Hot Tin Roof (1958) we can toss in scantily-clad, sexually starved southern belles who lurk alluringly by the roadside offering moonshine - sirens of the Southland seducing men and then betraying them for money.

From Coal Miners Daughter (1986) we can draw images of ramshackle shacks hanging perilously off steep hillsides, papered with pages from Sears catalogues, the overall-weaving inhabitants chewing tobacco as they gather around the radio playing the 'Grand Old Opry' on a Saturday night.

From Mississippi Burning (1988) we can absorb visions of the Ku Klux Klan, enormously powerful, brilliantly menacing in its cross-burning, white robed, head-covered ten-thousand-member fullness, infiltrating the political, judicial and law enforcement functions of Southern society, merging The Blob and Invasion of the Body Snatchers in an unholy alliance.

And finally, there are encounters with Southern Christianity a lá Jim and Tammy Faye Baker and Jimmy Swaggert. Southern spirituality is understood as swerving between mindless, blind faith in cleansing and redemption rituals taking place in murky rivers and flagrantly corrupt, violent and monstrous Bible purveyors: men who make a damn good living selling the Good Book.

These are not the poetic images of the Odyssey. They are the Coen Brothers' visions of Hell, which is spelled SOUTH.

Salvation in Sorrow

And yet, out of all this sorrow, the film brings salvation. Ulysses, we finally come to see, is actually quite happy being miserable. His wife and daughters' continual doubting of his abilities and competencies as a husband and father keep him grounded. He is most comfortable constantly struggling to keep his head above water. The least corrupt of the corrupt politicians is returned to the governorship of Mississippi, promising to utilize the services of Ulysses in his 'brain trust.' This governor, though obese, egocentric and self-aggrandizing is, at least, not a racist or anti-Semite.

DelMar, slow of thought but true of heart, Ulysses' loyal mariner and fellow traveller, acquires the money he needs to buy back his family's farm, because 'You ain't no kind of man, if you ain't got land.'

And the South, cleansed and saved by the purifying flood of TVA water, is 'electrified' and brought into the modern world: 'Maybe sometime ya'll, we'll be almost as good as New York.'

Notes
1 *Among these are* Blood Simple *(1984),* Raising Arizona *(1987), and* Fargo *(1996).*

[45]

The Ambi-Diegesis Of My Funny Valentine *Morris B. Holbrook*

My Funny Valentine [M.Damon 1998, M. Pfeiffer 1989] / The Fablous Baker Boys [Coppola 1979] & The Talented Mr Ripley [Mingella 1979]

The Ambi-Diegesis Of 'My Funny Valentine'

Morris B. Holbrook

Ambi-Diegesis

Diegetic and Non-Diegetic Film Music

Film scholars who address the cinematic role of music (Chion, 1994; Gabbard, 1996; Gorbman, 1987; Kalinak, 1992; Kassabian, 2001; Metz, 1974; Monaco, 1981; Smith, 1998; Tan, 1996) often distinguish between its diegetic uses (produced within the film as a natural part of the narrative action denoted on-screen) and its non-diegetic manifestations (produced externally by a source outside the film's denoted narrative action). Such commentators generally assume that diegetic music serves primarily to reinforce the realistic depiction of the mise-en-scène so as to enhance the verisimilitude of the narrative action in a manner comparable to that achieved by appropriate costumes, décor, scenery, or landscaping. By contrast, they assume that non-diegetic music contributes to a film's dramatic development by fleshing out a character, developing a theme, signalling an impending event, or otherwise drawing on associations and identifications that add depth to the meaning of a motion picture (Chion, 1994; Gorbman, 1987; Smith, 1998; see also Buhler, Flinn, and Neumeyer, ed., 2000).

Ambi-Diegetic Film Music

As various observers have noted, however, many uses of music in films blur the boundaries of the diegetic/non-diegetic distinction or fall between the extremes of these polarities (Altman, 1987; Chion, 1994; Kassabian, 2001; Smith, 1998; see also Buhler, et al., ed., 2000). One such possibility, not specifically emphasized by others, involves the use of film music in a manner that I would characterize as ambi-diegetic (Holbrook, 2002). Here, I refer to a cinematic situation in which a character actually performs a tune or song on camera (within the image) in a way that adds depth to that character by forming persona-related associations, that elaborates on thematic aspects of the plot, or that advances relevant symbolic identifications so as to enrich the meaning of the scene (dramatic development). Conceptually, as elaborated by Holbrook (2002), the basis for defining ambi-diegetic film music stems from a cross-classification of the two key distinctions normally conflated in discussions of music in motion pictures - namely, diegetic versus non-diegetic music and the functions of realistic depiction versus dramatic development. Reflecting the terminology variously favoured by Chion (1994, bold letters) and by Kassabian (2001, italics), the relevant typology of film music appears in figure 1.

As indicated by this typology, the hitherto neglected category of ambi-diegetic music includes those types of film music that are produced within the visualized zone lying inside the film's figure 1

	Internal to Story World (Screen Music) *Realistic Depiction*	External to Story World *Dramatic Development*
Acousmatic Zone (Source Absent from Image) *Produced Outside – Nondiegetic*	Offscreen Music *In–Between Music*	**Nondiegetic** Pit Music *Nondiegetic Music*
Visualized Zone (Source Present in Image) *Produced Inside – Diegetic*	Onscreen Music *Diegetic Music*	***AMBI-DIEGETIC MUSIC***

imaged action (as when a character performs a song on-screen) but that play an important role in the external aspects of the film's dramatic development (as when this musical performance sheds light on the character's motivations or provides associations that identify important aspects of the plot, setting, or key thematic ideas).

[49]

Illustration

The most obvious examples of such ambi-diegetic film music appear in the traditional Hollywood musical - a genre of film music that, with rare exceptions (Altman, 1987; Feuer, 1993), has been neglected by those working in this area of film criticism (Smith, 1998, p. 21; Rodman, 2000, p. 188). Elsewhere and even more frequently, comparable ambi-diegetic uses of songs show up in all sorts of films that fall outside the 'musical' genre and that are typically classified as dramas, comedies, mysteries, action adventures, sci-fi fantasies, westerns, or whatever.

The primary illustration of ambi-diegetic film music pursued here involves musical performances found in two recent motion pictures - The Fabulous Baker Boys (1989) and The Talented Mr. Ripley (1999). By way of example I will focus attention on the role in both films played by Rodgers-and-Hart's My Funny Valentine (1937) - first, in developing the image of Susie Diamond (Michelle Pfeiffer) as a sexy saloon singer; second and by contrast, in portraying the character of Tom Ripley (Matt Damon) as a self-absorbed, sociopathic, sexually ambivalent wastrel.

Acting Tradition

Face it: Many actors and actresses cannot carry a tune, much less sing with distinction, so that dubbing in the voices of accomplished singers is an age-old practice (Tormé, 1994, pp. 185-188).

Yet some movie stars nonetheless dig deep within their wells of creativity to produce credible singing performances. In the present case, Michelle Pfeiffer establishes her credentials as a viable real-life torch singer with considerable dramatic plausibility, while Matt Damon manages a commendably sincere evocation of an enigmatically effete but undeniably compelling vocal stylist.

History of the Song's Past Appearances

Beyond this, the song My Funny Valentine *carries connotations associated with a long history of appearances in a wide variety of entertainment venues. Written in 1937 by Richard Rodgers and Lorenz Hart for their Broadway show entitled* Babes In Arms, *the song originally limned the foibles of a slightly 'dopey' individual named Valentine or Val (Friedwald, 2002, p. 354; Hyland, 1995, p. 238; Nolan, 1994, p. 217). But* My Funny Valentine *has since come to serve as a generic bittersweet love call to anyone seen as a suitable target for one's romantic affections.*

Wilder (1972) reports on the iconic stature of My Funny Valentine *as a favourite late-night cocktail-lounge torch song and considers the piece 'as finely distilled a theatre song as I have ever heard' (p. 207). Meanwhile, Furia (1992) explicates the lyrics to* My Funny Valentine - *finding the song to be a triumph of 'unobtrusive rhyming,' 'skewed flattery,' and affectionate 'disproportions' (p. 119). More recently Friedwald (2002) shows how this song achieves the ideal of 'matching text to music' (p. 358) - first, in the way 'the major/minor nature of the music' brilliantly mirrors 'the happy/sad nature of the lyric' (p. 360); second, in the way the word 'open' is accompanied by a startling leap in the melodic line; and third, in the way the high note on 'stay' lingers poignantly for a full two measures.*

While listening to the sensitive, finely tuned lyrics to My Funny Valentine, *we might gain some further perspective on the meanings packed into its poetry by contemplating the poignantly sad nature of the gifted man who wrote them (Nolan, 1994). Larry Hart happened to be a five-foot, homosexual, alcoholic, cigar-smoking, chubby, bald-headed, misshapen, dishevelled, mirror-avoiding dwarf who died, officially of pneumonia but basically of self-neglect, at the age of forty-eight. The challenge to a performer of* My Funny Valentine *is to capture the essence of the tragedy that lurks below its surface.*

Over the years, My Funny Valentine *has been part of the repertoire of sophisticated pop and jazz artists icons and been covered by a diverse range of performers-from Ella Fitzgerald to Miranda Sex Garden. Over six-hundred such versions currently exist on compact disc.*

Associations with Earlier Iconic Performers

Central to the fundamental structure of this essay, we must further emphasize three major musical connections that appear especially salient to the associations identified with My Funny Valentine.

These involve strong imaginative links of this song with the careers and personalities of three key performers - Frank Sinatra, Kim Novak, and Chet Baker.

Frank Sinatra

This is not the place to list Frank Sinatra musical accomplishments, nor to give a fully-detailed account of his encounters with a piece such as My Funny Valentine *in particular, which he recorded several times during his long career.*

Suffice to say that Sinatra and My Funny Valentine *are indelibly connected in the minds of music fans everywhere. Most commentators would place him as the reigning authority, the definitive interpreter of popular and jazz-oriented songs such as* My Funny Valentine *(Friedwald, 1990, p. 320; Friedwald, 1995, p. 157; Petkov, 1995, p. 79; Rockwell, 1984, p. 81; Wilder, 1972, p. 147) 'owning' one approach to singing* My Funny Valentine *featuring detailed attention to the minute nuances of the lyrics, impeccable intonation, precise articulation, carefully controlled breathing - in short, the approach reflecting vocal musicianship of the highest order dedicated to the purpose of creating a warmly glowing romantic bond with the listener (Friedwald, 1995, pp. 18-55; Lees, 1987, pp. 104-115; Mustazza, 1995, p. 5; Pleasants, 1974, pp. 187-196; Rockwell, 1984, p. 52).*

More specifically pertinent to this essay, Sinatra participated as Kim Novak's and Rita Hayworth's love interest(s) in George Sidney's film version of Pal Joey *(1957). Here, he didn't get to sing* My Funny Valentine - *but did get to sit there on-screen while Hayworth watched him watching Novak (lip-synching Trudi Ewen) perform it in highly-inviting spot-lit splendour.*

[51]

On up-tempo tunes, Sinatra adopted the 'hard-swinging, heterosexual approach' (Friedwald, 1995, p. 285) loaded with aggressively animated 'charismatic Sinatra virility' (p. 312). But on ballads such as Valentine, *he epitomized his self-described category of 'saloon singer' (Lees, 1987, p. 113) - perfecting a tender, wistful, forlorn style of singing (Friedwald, 1995, p. 312) that smoulders with passion presented in a compellingly personal delivery in which the singer's gender-specific characteristics appear with the fullest possible force as quintessentially masculine for a male singer such as Sinatra or as quintessentially feminine for a female lip-syncher such as Kim Novak.*

Kim Novak

Playing the role of the 'nice' chorus girl Linda English in Pal Joey, *Kim Novak performs* My Funny Valentine *in a manner that positions her, appropriately enough, as firmly occupying the distaff side of the image associated with Sinatra as the uncouth womanizer Joey Evans. In this featured number, while Joey/Frank watches, Linda/Kim is assertive, extroverted and self-confident, yet alluringly soft and coquettishly feminine. Though she does not actually sing the notes to*

'Valentine' in her own voice, she acts the part with utter conviction and lip-synchs to perfection, achieving a verisimilitude exceeding that often accomplished by real singers miming their own voices (including, by the way, Sinatra himself in this particular film). The chemistry between Linda/Kim and Joey/Frank practically jumps off the screen and bolsters rumours that the two were having a real-life affair at about this time (Newsweek, 1965, ed., 1995, p. 94).

Though usually abstemious, in one scene Linda/Kim mimics the fondness of Sinatra - whom Rockwell (1984) characterizes as 'the archetypal balladeer of ... the 'booze sensibility'' (p. 162) - for alcohol, rather than hard drugs, as his intoxicant of choice. Specifically, Linda/Kim goes in an inebriated state to visit Joey/Frank. Instead of taking advantage of her spectacular but defenceless charms, Frank treats Kim with admirably restrained paws-off gallantry. Such relatively responsible use of controlled substances contrasts vividly with the harrowing experiences of Chet Baker.

Chet Baker

An alternative approach to My Funny Valentine *appeared in the roughly contemporaneous work of the trumpeter and vocalist Chet Baker. Baker first recorded two uniquely personal versions of the piece on trumpet for Fantasy and Pacific Jazz while playing with the Gerry Mulligan Quartet in 1952 and 1953, respectively. Baker's work on the horn is dark, sombre, brooding, gently sad, and wistfully tentative. He had a flair for seeming constantly on the brink of losing his place or hitting a clinker, but somehow - magically - always managing to come up with the perfect note instead. Musically, on* Valentine, *as in much of his playing, Chet sounds like a man on the verge of a nervous breakdown.*

[52]

These suspicions intensified when Baker recorded a vocal version of the song with his own quartet featuring Russ Freeman on piano in 1954 for Pacific Jazz. Here, he sings in a high, effeminate voice - clearly, the antithesis of Sinatra's macho vocal style - vulnerable, fragile, introverted, epicene in the extreme, yet deeply penetrating and disturbingly compelling.

On trumpet - though largely autodidactic, primarily intuitive, barely able to read music, harmonically illiterate, loathe to practice, and limited in technique to the middle register of the horn - Baker was nonetheless a superb musician with a completely distinct sound all his own, crackling on up-tempo tunes and sweetly pure on slower ballads. The latter qualities also informed his uniquely insightful and poignant singing style - soft but pure, effete but honest, delicate but clear as a bell, well-crafted in breath control, and always deadly accurate in his pitch-perfect intonation (Friedwald, 1990, pp. 367-368; Valk, 1989, pp. 229-230; Zwerin, 1981). Summing up these qualities, Carr, Case, and Dellar (1986) explain how Chet laid the definitive My Funny Valentine: *'His melancholy tone and simple lyricism seemed to linger in the nerve endings long after the last note had sounded... And his voice cast the same forlorn, little-boy-lost shadow' (p. 80). Chet Baker recorded* My Funny Valentine *on countless occasions. (Friedwald, 2002). Each rendition over the years revealed Chet's defining sense of vulnerability, ambivalent longing and androgynous openness. Baker's musical persona may have presaged various psychological traits that led him down a path of self-destruction - his struggle with a life-long dependency on drugs and alcohol and died tragically, falling out of a hotel window.*

During his lifetime, Chet Baker appeared in a number of motion pictures - as both musician and actor - perhaps most fittingly, in Robert Altman's The James Dean Story *(1957) which features his haunting trumpet solos, where he sounds especially moody and mournful on a background piece called* Let Me Be Loved. *If there is such a thing as crying through the horn, this is it.*

These qualities also appear with painful clarity in a totally depressing photo-documentary made by the sometime fashion photographer Bruce Weber under the title Let's Get Lost *(1989). Herein, Baker - whose handsome looks once inspired flattering comparisons with the likes of James Dean - emerges as a haunted shadow of his former self, a hopeless junky, a man devoid of self-respect who has alienated almost everyone who ever cared about him. Weber specializes in juxtaposing photos of the once-beautiful twenty-four-year-old trumpeter - especially those taken by the brilliant West Coast photographer William Claxton (1993) - with shots of Baker as a fifty-eight-year-old, frail, denture-wearing lifetime drug addict. The early Chet was good-looking enough to become a poster boy for hipness(Carr et al., 1986) - the older Baker looks in every way as if he already has one foot in the grave - which, as it happens, he does.*

[53]

These human and musical qualities get reincarnated in Baker's posthumous contributions to two films - namely, L.A. Confidential *(1997) and* Playing By Heart *(1998). As explained by Curtis Hanson in a promotional piece that introduces the VHS videotape of his film,* L.A. Confidential *uses ambi-diegetic jazz to provide a musical context that delineates key characters in the motion picture. Indeed, music by Chet Baker limns the corruption, seediness, and depravity embodied by some rather unsavoury central figures.*

Summary and Preview
The comparisons just suggested follow from a consideration of three different approaches to music in general and to performing My Funny Valentine *in particular. They may be construed as suggesting that Kim Novak takes the Frank Sinatra approach in one direction (toward the distaff side), whereas Chet Baker pushes the Sinatra model along another path (toward the androgynous edge). By way of summary and preview, this pattern of homologous relationships appears as follows:*

Baker Boys and Mr. Ripley
Clearly, then, My Funny Valentine *comes to its recent use in films with a great deal of imaginative baggage attached. Such associations and identifications inform our experience of hearing*

Michelle Pfeiffer perform Valentine *in* The Fabulous Baker Boys *(1989) and watching Matt Damon sing the song in* The Talented Mr. Ripley *(1999).*

Michelle Pfeiffer in The Fabulous Baker Boys

Clearly, Michelle Pfeiffer draws on the tradition of My Funny Valentine *as a torch song lip-synched by Kim Novak in* Pal Joey. *In this connection, Pfeiffer reports at fabulous bakers.tripod.com that she listened to performances by Billie Holiday, Dinah Washington, Sarah Vaughan, and Helen Merrill in preparing for her role as the world-weary ex-escort-service saloon-singing bombshell Susie Diamond. Michelle's own-voice rendition of* Valentine *- vividly reinforced by the recollected imagery of her strikingly erotic piano-top choreography on* Makin' Whoopee *earlier in the film - reflects her carefully cultivated persona as a sexy, showgirl with the assertive-yet-soft, extroverted, self-confidently feminine qualities associated with the* Valentine-*enhanced Kim Novak persona. On the Baker Boys Website, Pfeiffer further describes her characterization of ex-hooker Susie Diamond as 'trashy, cocky and real smart.' The film's writer/director Steve Kloves adds that 'These songs were chosen because they ...reflect the characters, I think.' It is this character-reflecting aspect of ambi-diegetic film music that we emphasize in the present discussion.*

[54]

Besides Susie/Michelle, the relevant participants include the real-life brothers Jeff and Beau Bridges as Jack and Frank Baker - a pair of fraternal partners in a dual-piano lounge act that features such cocktail-circuit favourites as People, The Girl from Ipanema, *and* You're Sixteen (You're Beautiful and You're Mine). *The ambi-diegetic tunes just mentioned capture the essence of the schmaltzy musical personality evinced by the older brother Frank/Beau (dubbed by John F. Hammond on piano), whose limitations as a musician are exceeded only by his burdensome sense of responsibility as an income-earning family man - sincerely dedicated to the reality principle and therefore subservient in every respect to the commercial, entertaining, audience-pandering, money-grubbing side of the lounge-act business. By contrast, little brother Jack/Jeff (dubbed on piano by the film's talented music director Dave Grusin and meticulously hand-synched by Jeff Bridges throughout) expresses his own musical personality in three scenes when he retreats, first, to a piano in an abandoned restaurant; second, to a collaboration with bass-and-drums accompaniment at Henry's jazz club in Seattle; and, third, to a solo performance at the same club. In these ambi-diegetic moments, Jack/Jeff plays a form of highly sophisticated, lyrically cerebral jazz of the type most closely associated with the influence of Bill Evans. We sense his intense but lonely absorption in this music and feel the enormity of the loss implicit in his submission to the aesthetically vacant chores of a schlock-pandering cocktail-lounge pianist. Alas, Jack/Jeff remains trapped by his brotherly contract with Frank/Beau - knowing that his older brother could not sustain a decent livelihood without him and therefore submitting to this painful arrangement, even at the cost of sacrificing his own artistic creativity. Meanwhile, he adopts a cynical posture and, subservient to the pleasure principle, evinces a strong propensity toward womanizing. In short,* The Fabulous Baker Boys *embody a clearly structured series of parallel binary oppositions, reflected in summary form by the following set of homologous comparisons:*

Frank/Beau - Jack/Jeff
Business - Aesthetics
Entertainment - Art
Commerce - Creativity
Reality Principle - Pleasure Principle
Responsibility - Freedom
Sincere - Cynical
Family Man - Loner
Faithful - Womanizing
Head - Heart
Money - Love
Schlock Pop - Jazz

This precarious balancing act begins to crumble when the Baker Brothers realize that, to bolster their flagging popular appeal, they need to supplement their act with the added attraction of a girl singer. They audition thirty-seven young women and the thirty-eighth applicant turns out to be Susie/Michelle, who arrives late and cheerfully admits she has no previous singing experience, but whose compelling performance of More Than You Know *is more than promising enough to land her the job of girl singer in this or virtually any other cabaret or lounge act.*

[55]

Note the subtle distinction between 'cabaret' and 'lounge.' The first implies taste and refinement. The second suggests schlock and sleaziness. Indeed, with the addition of Susie/Michelle and the careful polishing of her rough edges by brother Frank/Beau (who buys her some slinky clothes and coaches her not to say 'fuck' on the open microphone), The Fabulous Baker Boys *plus Susie Diamond transmogrify from the lowly status of a lounge act to the more exalted stature of a cabaret attraction.*

When Frank/Beau must leave the posh resort and return home for a family emergency, Jack/Jeff and Susie/Michelle make love after she has delivered a stunning and much-celebrated ambi-diegetic version of Makin' Whoopee. *In this seductive performance, Susie/Michelle wears a sexy red dress that rides up to just ever so slightly below her crotch as she sprawls atop the Steinway grand and slithers around suggestively while Jack/Jeff supplies an inspired gospel-tinged piano accompaniment hand-synched to perfection by Bridges miming Grusin in case anyone is watching). This sampling of ambi-diegetic jazz - so powerful in conveying Susie/Michelle's character of Susie/Michelle - has become something of a cult classic.*

Most meaningful in pointing to the immanent dissolution of the trio is a discussion by the three major protagonists of Feelings *- that much-despised warhorse of the cocktail circuit, beloved to lounge lizards everywhere. Susie/Michelle voices the case for aesthetically grounded artistic integrity by declaring that it is not fun to sing* Feelings *and wondering aloud whether anyone really needs to hear this trite piece ever again. Frank/Beau replies defensively that* Feelings *is a key part of their act and that they have a responsibility to perform it for the audiences who have paid good money to hear it. Tellingly, Susie/Michelle replies that, to her,* Feelings *is like parsley. This musical insight apparently motivates the lacklustre manner in which she delivers* Feelings *in the next scene, with sloppy phrasing and pointed body language that vividly convey her complete lack of involvement with the piece and its performance. After this revelatory ambi-diegetic musical episode, Susie/Michelle announces her intention to quit the group immediately to pursue an alternative opportunity in making cat-food commercials. Her departure precipitates a monumental lovers' quarrel with Jack/Jeff, raising questions about the fate of their relationship.*

In the movie's final scene, Jack/Jeff pays a visit to Susie/Michelle. What next transpires has prompted several critics and commentators to opine that the future of the couple's relationship is left hanging by the film's conclusion and remains in doubt. Such an interpretation depends on cleaving to the literal meaning of the verbal exchange that occurs between the hero and heroine while ignoring the dramatic development conveyed in part by their body language and especially by the film's music.

[56]

If we attend to nothing but the literal meaning in their dialogue, we might possibly experience uncertainty over whether this couple will reunite. For - beyond the little facial nuances and expressive gestures so well-conveyed by Susie/Michelle and Jack/Jeff in this concluding scene - what happens next gives the clearest possible signal of an impending romantic reconciliation. Specifically, as Susie/Michelle walks away, a new kind of background music begins to play. One lone piano (unmistakably, Jack/Jeff) accompanies some humming (obviously, Susie/Michelle). As we, the camera, and Jack/Jeff watch Susie/Michelle strolling down the street, she begins her sensitively gentle rendition of ... My Funny Valentine. *While Susie/Michelle continues to sing to the piano accompaniment by Jack/Jeff, an orchestra joins in as the film fades to black and the credits begin to roll. We cannot conceivably doubt that we are privileged to eavesdrop on a preview of the renewed relationship that will soon reunite this couple in song. And, when Susie/Michelle works her way toward the powerful concluding phrase in which she implores her lover Jack/Jeff to 'stay ... stay,' the film credits reach the moment at which they announce the role of Dave Grusin in dubbing the piano performances by Jeff Bridges, and we are left with the prescient reminder that, as Richard Rodgers and Lorenz Hart have been insisting for over six decades, every day is Valentine's Day.*

Matt Damon in Mr. Ripley

Meanwhile, drawing on another side of the My Funny Valentine *iconography and playing the title role of Tom Ripley in Anthony* English Patient *Minghella's* The Talented Mr. Ripley *(1999), Matt Damon emulates the enigmatically effete singing style of Chet Baker, a venture in which he receives valuably convincing assistance from some lyrically cool Baker-like trumpet work by Guy Barker. Baker's qualities of sensitive sadness, stubborn self-destructiveness, and sexual ambiguity transfer to the character played by Damon and prove proleptic of the developments in that character still to come in subsequent portions of the motion picture. Indeed, the film's full title - which flashes by very quickly, almost subliminally, during its opening credits - captures the Chet Baker persona as accurately as it does that of the Ripley/Damon character: the mysterious, yearning, sensitive, sad, lonely, troubled, confused, loving, musical, gifted, intelligent, beautiful, tender, sensitive, haunted, passionate, talented Mr. Ripley.*

Shot in parts of Italy frequented by Chet Baker himself during the 1950s, the film makes explicit connections between Ripley/Damon and the troubled singer. At one point, Tom/Matt drops a stack of records and Chet's classic Chet Baker Sings *album on Pacific Jazz comes out on top. As noted by Gavin (2002), Baker has become 'a world-wide myth': 'The original* Chet Baker Sings *album held a mystique for all generations' (p. 378). Relying in part on Ripley/Damon's physiognomic resemblance to the pretty-boy image of Baker during the 1950s, director Minghella stages Tom/Matt's performance of* My Funny Valentine *at a crowded, smoke-filled, neon-enhanced, slightly seedy nightclub in Naples called Hot Jazz Vesuvio, where the actor sings the song 'very much in the mood of Chet Baker.' Quoted at www.talentedmrripley.com, Minghella explains:*

> Music is at the heart of the film... I thought about what was particular to the period (the 1950s), existentialism and jazz... Eventually the film demonstrates that ... Ripley is the one who can genuinely, almost pathologically improvise. That is his talent. Ripley is a master at it, the real anarchist and subverter... More than anything else, it's Chet Baker that makes you feel the late '50s.

On the same Website, Matt Damon confesses that 'Basically, I just imitated Chet Baker('s) singing as best I could.'

Using these associations as an imaginative basis, Minghella builds up Ripley/Damon's homosexual inclinations and sociopathic tendencies beyond those found in the original Patricia Highsmith novel. Much as I happen to admire Chet Baker's singing, the connective link between Tom/Matt and Chet works powerfully to advance the developing relationship - first homoerotic, then lethal - between Tom Ripley (Matt Damon) and Dickie Greenleaf (Jude Law). Via this associative connection, tragedy or at least pathology is identified with the fifty-year-old image of a jazz icon and maybe even with the doomed lyricist who penned his most celebrated song (Friedwald, 2002, p. 371).

The expressive use of ambi-diegetic music in Mr. Ripley supports the main outlines of its intricate plot. At the film's beginning, we find Tom/Matt playing piano accompaniment for an operatic singer at a recital on the terrace of a Fifth Avenue penthouse overlooking Central Park in New York. Ripley/Damon works as a men's room attendant, but dabbles in classical piano on the side. The party's filthy-rich host - Herbert Richard Greenleaf (James Rebhorn) - mistakes him for a friend of his picaresque playboy Princetonian son Dickie (Jude Law) and employs Tom/Matt to travel to Italy to try to convince the wayward Dickie/Jude to return home.

Realizing that he will need to charm young Greenleaf/Law and knowing that Dickie/Jude loves jazz, Ripley/Damon studies up on this alien art form. As a classical aficionado - like the elder Greenleaf/Rebhorn - Ripley/Damon hates this music. He especially dislikes My Funny Valentine *by Chet Baker and comments that he can't even tell if it is sung by a man or a woman.*

Arriving in Italy and showing a Baker-like tendency toward deceit, Tom/Matt is soon spying on Dickie/Jude and his fiancée Marge Sherwood (Gwyneth Paltrow) as they cavort on Dickie's sailboat. Gradually, Tom/Matt arranges to meet the young couple and insinuates himself into their good graces. Ironically enough and further reminiscent of Chet Baker, Ripley/Damon openly admits that he is a fraud - expert in forging signatures and imitating others - which he proves by performing a dead-on vocal impression of the elder Greenleaf/Rebhorn. In private, he also accurately mimics Marge/Gwyneth and Dickie/Jude talking about himself. But nowhere does his flair for imitation exceed that which he invests in duplicitously pretending to be a jazz fan - his strategy for charming Dickie/Jude. Thus, on the point of being forced to leave the company of Marge and Dickie, Tom/Matt 'accidentally' drops the contents of his briefcase, which include several jazz albums by the likes of Sonny Rollins and John Coltrane plus - coming out on the top of the stack - Chet Baker Sings. *Dickie/Jude becomes especially excited to see the Baker recording and, to show his enthusiasm, takes Tom/Matt to his favourite jazz club, Hot Jazz Vesuvio, in Naples. Besides enhancing the impression of Dickie/Jude as a good-time party boy, this episode is most notable for illustrating the effortless naturalness with which Ripley/Damon can blend seamlessly into virtually any musical environment.*

Soon, Tom/Matt gets an opportunity to impress Dickie/Jude even further by virtue of his striking emulation of Chet Baker on My Funny Valentine. *Interestingly, though this performance ends ambi-diegetically, it begins as a non-diegetic part of the musical score. Specifically, over what at first sounds like Chet Baker's muted trumpet in the background, we watch Marge/Gwyneth and Tom/Matt walk together through a village street while Marge/Gwyneth describes how she met Dickie/Jude when he used to play* My Funny Valentine *on his alto sax at a small café in Paris.*

At this exact moment in the dialogue, we hear what sounds like Chet Baker enter vocally with the first words of the song's lyrics. Marge/Gwyneth says she later discovered that Dickie/Jude only knows about six songs. While the music proceeds, Marge/Gwyneth and Tom/Matt buy some fruit; watch Dickie/Jude playing bocci; banter with Dickie/Jude about getting together at 7:00 pm; and later meet Dickie/Jude again for a motor-scooter ride back to the jazz club in Naples, where we now ambi-diegetically watch what turns out to our surprise to be Tom/Matt himself singing just the last eight bars in his impressively accurate impersonation of Chet Baker - with Dickie/Jude listening appreciatively and then playing an accompaniment on alto, rounded out by the muted Chet-like trumpet of Guy Barker. Here, except for smiling more than Chet would have approved, Ripley/Damon does a terrific job of mimicry - admirably capturing the haunted Baker persona.

Of course, Tom/Matt also manages to charm the pants off the appreciative Dickie/Jude - whom we soon encounter naked in the bathtub, playing chess with the more-and-more openly homoerotic Ripley/Damon. Tom/Matt even asks if he can get in the tub - a thought that apparently fills Dickie/Jude with homophobic horror. But, blinded by passion, Ripley/Damon misinterprets these cues and - starting from such early misconceptions - develops a crush on Greenleaf/Law from which the rest of the film's intricately convoluted plot lines begin to unfold.

Before long, when Dickie/Jude announces that he wants to break off their relationship, Tom/Matt is horrified and responds by bludgeoning Greenleaf/Law to death. From that point on, adding immeasurably to the complexity of the plot, Ripley/Damon begins to impersonate Dickie/Jude with some people while remaining Tom/Matt with others. This double identity involves all sorts of intricate duplicities, shameless lies, phony letters, forged signatures, purloined passports, cloak-and-dagger intrigues and killings. Inevitably, the intertwined threads of Ripley's deceptions get increasingly ensnarled and difficult to sustain, culminating in the brutal murder of his soul-mate lover Peter Smith-Kingsley (Jack Davenport).

[59]

These traits are well-suited to a character drawn with the help of associations and identifications borrowed from the tragic image of the prototypical lost soul Chet Baker and the two personas - Tom and Chet - do share many qualities of character in common. Both are basically vulnerable, fragile, introverted, self-destructive, androgynous, sociopathic misfits. Recall, for example, that Chet Baker served more than his fair share of time in jail (Gavin 2002; Valk 1989) - often for forgery when he signed doctors' names to phony drug prescriptions, forgery being a specialty that Ripley/Damon has also mastered.

So Ripley/Damon's adroit impersonation - that is, his deadly accurate imitation of Chet Baker singing My Funny Valentine *- builds a set of imaginative associations vital to conveying the complexity of his mysterious yearning sensitive sad lonely troubled confused loving musical gifted intelligent beautiful tender sensitive haunted" but ever so "passionate" and above all "talented"* *nature. As noted earlier, in the film, the first twenty-four bars of Ripley/Damon's performance serve as nondiegetic background music, with only the last eight bars appearing in the form of Damon's ambi-diegetic performance at the Naples jazz club. But when preparing the video released by Sony Classical (www.talentedmrripley.com), Minghella & Co. covered the whole performance of the piece by Matt at the "Hot Jazz Vesuvio" with scattered snatches from the film intermixed in a montage. Viewed at amplified length, the fidelity of Damon's impersonation of Chet Baker becomes more impressive than ever. Without actually achieving the purity of Baker's sound or the accuracy of his intonation, Damon has managed to capture the essence of his vocal mannerisms.*

All this attains even greater significance if we contemplate for a moment the piece that serves as something of a theme song for The Talented Mr. Ripley. *Specifically, three times during the course of the film, we hear the meaning-laden tune* You Don't Know What Love Is. *Dickie/Jude plays it on his alto sax just after he has witnessed the grim aftermath of a suicide for which, it turns out, he is largely responsible. A lone tenor saxophonist intones the piece on a corner in Venice outside the café where Ripley/Damon meets the grief-struck and guilt-ridden elder Greenleaf/ Rebhorn.*

Since its introduction by Carol Bruce in an Abbott-and-Costello film called Keep 'Em Flying *(1941), Raye and DePaul's* You Don't Know What Love Is *has been recorded by countless singers in innumerable contexts from Tony Bennett to Cassandra Wilson- though, amazingly, not Frank Sinatra. However, the hands-down classic vocal and instrumental recording of this song - the most darkly broodingreading, the one you hear ubiquitously today in bars, restaurants, nightclubs, and stage productions all over Los Angeles and New York City - was recorded long ago by someone very close to the essence of Mr. Ripley. Specifically, in 1955. For Pacific Jazz. With Russ Freeman on piano, Carson Smith on bass, and Bob Neel on drums. By none other than ... Chet Baker.*

References

Altman, Rick (1987), *The American Film Musical*, Bloomington, IN: Indiana University Press.

Baker, Chet (1997), *As Though I Had Wings: The Lost Memoir*, New York, NY: St. Martin's Press.

Buhler, James, Caryl Flinn, and David Neumeyer (ed. 2000), *Music and Cinema*, Hanover, NH: Wesleyan University Press.

Carr, Roy, Brian Case, and Fred Dellar (1986), *The Hip: Hipsters, Jazz and the Beat Generation*, London, UK: Faber and Faber.

Chion, Michel (1994), *Audio-Vision: Sound on Screen*, ed. and trans. Claudia Gorbman, New York, NY: Columbia University Press.

Claxton, William (1993), *Young Chet*, London, UK: Schirmer Art Books.

Feuer, Jane (1993), *The Hollywood Musical*, Bloomington, IN: Indiana University Press.

Furia, Philip (1992), *The Poets of Tin Pan Alley: A History of America's Great Lyricists*, New York, NY: Oxford University Press.

Frank, Alan (1978), *Sinatra*, New York, NY: Leon Amiel Publisher.

Friedwald, Will (1990), *Jazz Singing: America's Great Voices from Bessie Smith to Bebop and Beyond*, New York, NY: Charles Scribner's Sons.

Friedwald, Will (1995), *Sinatra! The Song Is You: A Singer's Art*, New York, NY: Scribner.

Friedwald, Will (2002), *Stardust Melodies: The Biography of Twelve of America's Most Popular Songs*, New York, NY: Pantheon Books.

Furia, Philip (1992), *The Poets of Tin Pan Alley: A History of America's Greatest Lyricists*, New York, NY: Oxford University Press.

Gabbard, Krin (1996), *Jammin' at the Margins: Jazz and the American Cinema*, Chicago, IL: The University of Chicago Press.

Gavin, James (2002), *Deep in a Dream: The Long Night of Chet Baker*, New York, NY: Alfred A. Knopf.

Gorbman, Claudia (1987), *Unheard Melodies: Narrative Film Music*, Bloomington, IN: Indiana University Press.

Holbrook, Morris B. (2002), *"A Book-Review Essay on the Role of Ambi-Diegetic Film Music in the Product Design of Hollywood Movies: Macromarketing in LA-LA-Land,"* Working Paper, Graduate School of Business, Columbia University.

Hyland , William G. (1995), *The Song Is Ended: Songwriters and American Music,* 1900-1950, New York, NY: Oxford University Press.

Kalinak, Kathryn (1992), *Settling the Score: Music and the Classical Hollywood Film*, Madison, WI: University of Wisconsin Press.

Kassabian, Anahid (2001), *Hearing Film: Tracking Identifications in Contemporary Hollywood Film Music*, New York, NY: Routledge.

Lees, Gene (1985), *"Frank Sinatra,"* booklet/essay for Frank Sinatra, *Time-Life Music Series on Legendary Singers*, New York, NY: Time-Life Books.

Lees, Gene (1987), *Singers and the Song*, New York, NY: Oxford University Press.

Metz, Christian (1974), *Film Language: A Semiotics of the Cinema*, New York, NY: Oxford University Press.

Monaco, James (1981), *How to Read a Film: The Art, Technology, Language, History, and Theory of Film and Media, Revised Edition*, New York, NY: Oxford University Press.

Moody, Bill (2002), *Looking For Chet Baker: An Evan Horne Mystery*, New York, NY: Walker & Company.

Mustazza, Leonard (1995), *"Introduction - Sinatra's Enduring Appeal: Art and Heart,"* in Petkov and Mustazza (ed. 1995), 3-10.

Newsweek (1965), "Sinatra: Where the Action Is," *Newsweek*, (September 6), 39-42. In Petkov and Mustazza (ed. 1995), 90-98.

Nolan, Frederick (1994), *Lorenz Hart: A Poet on Broadway*, New York, NY: Oxford University Press.

Petkov, Steven (1995), *"Ol' Blue Eyes and the Golden Age of the American Song: The Capitol years,"* in Petkov and Mustazza (ed. 1995), 74-84.

Petkov, Steven and Leonard Mustazza (ed. 1995), *The Sinatra Reader*, New York, NY: Oxford University Press.

Pleasants, Henry (1974), *The Great American Popular Singers*, New York, NY: Simon & Schuster.

Rockwell, John (1984), *Sinatra: An American Classic*, New York, NY: Random House.

Rodman, Ronald (2000), *"Tonal Design and the Aesthetic of Pastiche in Herbert Stothart's Maytime,"* in Buhler et al. (ed. 2000), 187-206.

Smith, Jeff (1998), *The Sounds of Commerce: Marketing Popular Film Music*, New York, NY: Columbia University Press.

Tan, Ed. S. (1996), *Emotion and the Structure of Narrative Film: Film as an Emotion Machine*, trans. Barbara Fasting, Mahwah, NJ: Lawrence Erlbaum.

Tormé, Mel (1994), *My Singing Teachers*, New York, NY: Oxford University Press.

Valk, Jeroen de (1989), *Chet Baker: His Life and Music,* Berkeley, CA: Berkeley Hills Books.

Wilder, Alec (1972), *American Popular Song: The Great Innovators, 1900-1950*, London, UK: Oxford University Press.

Wulff, Ingo (1989), *Chet Baker: In Concert*, Bremen, Germany: Nieswand Verlag.

Wulff, Ingo (1993), *Chet Baker in Europe: 1975-1988*, Bremen, Germany: Nieswand Verlag.

Zwerin, Mike (1981), *"The Tender Trumpet of Chet Baker,"* The International Herald Tribune, November 12.

Music, Masculinity & Membership *Ian Inglis*

Can't Take My Eyes Off You [Frankie Valli, 1967] / The Deer Hunter [Michael Cimino, 1978]

Music, Masculinity And Membership

Ian Inglis

The Deer Hunter *was the second film to be directed by Michael Cimino. After directing television commercials in New York for several years, he moved to Hollywood, where he was co-writer on the screenplays of* Silent Running *(Douglas Trumbull, 1971) and* Magnum Force *(Ted Post, 1973) before directing (and co-writing)* Thunderbolt And Lightfoot *(1974). Shot in America and Thailand,* The Deer Hunter *tells the story of a group of blue-collar workers in a Pennsylvania steel town, whose lives and friendships are disrupted by the experiences of three of the men in Vietnam. It was released in 1978 and won many international awards, including five Oscars - best film, director, supporting actor (Christopher Walken), film editing, and sound. However, in addition to its critical and commercial success, it generated considerable controversy and opposition, not least for its crude, racist depiction of the Vietnamese. As Adair has noted, 'Cimino's Viet Cong cannot even be called one-dimensional...they exist merely to objectify Occidental fears of the yellow race...they constitute an insult to the audience's intelligence' (1981, p. 139).*

[64]

The Deer Hunter *is also noteworthy for an unambiguous and broadly symmetrical structure, which separates the narrative into three segments. The first third of the film (sixty-four minutes) takes place in the town of Clairton, where the Russian-American community, from which the main characters are drawn, is preparing for a wedding; the second (forty minutes) chronicles the men's combat and subsequent captivity in Vietnam, and escape to Saigon; the final third (sixty-six minutes) is devoted to the group's attempts to resolve the consequences of the traumatic events in Vietnam.*

The first segment is remarkable in a film which is (ostensibly) characterised as a war movie, in that it says little about the war directly, but, for more than an hour, constructs a deeply-detailed and sentimentalised portrait of a tightly-knit community (in reality, a composite of eight different locations). Clairton appears untroubled by political, racial, economic or gender divisions. From the opening shot of a truck speeding through an urban-industrial landscape, it is apparent that this is an environment that has been constructed by and for men. The description by Auster & Quart illustrates its romanticised attributes:

> The boys labor in an almost mythic, tranquil world...they work with gusto and pleasure...they express no job resentment or alienation...Cimino's town emanates a feeling of back-slapping warmth, solidity, and full employment, and he augments those images with beautifully com-posed long shots of the silhouetted factory at dawn.

> *(1988, p. 62)*

At the end of their final night shift in the factory before their military service begins, Michael (Robert de Niro), Nick (Christopher Walken) and Steven (John Savage), accompanied by workmates Axel (Chuck Aspegren) and Stan (John Cazale), drive to the bar of another friend, John (George Dzundza). They are there to celebrate not only their impending departure but also Steven's wedding, later that day. It is this scene in the bar, just a few minutes into the film, that I wish to examine. Although relatively brief (less than three minutes), it contains behavioural and emotional elements which are explicitly and significantly revisited later in the film. In particular, it emphasises the structural and cultural components of the community; it suggests a homo-erotic tension between Michael and Nick; it effectively excludes women from the symbolic and material worlds inhabited by the men; it anchors the narrative to a particular place and time; it introduces the binary opposition between two worlds; it provides a bridge to the film's final scene; and through its observation of ritual it manifests a cohesive and enduring group membership. And it achieves much of this through the deliberate and strategic use of one piece of popular music.

As the men enter the already busy bar, it appears that they have merely moved from one all-male environment to another. The handshaking, joking and horseplay that marked their exit from the steel plant are continued without interruption. While the drinks - on the house - are served, they continue their banter, watch the football game on television, and bet with other customers on the outcome. When Stan shouts 'I got an extra twenty says the Eagles' quarterback wears a dress!' amid general merriment, it confirms that this is a community where approved modes of sexuality are aggressively upheld; indeed, the most common insult within the group is to refer to someone as a 'faggot'.

[65]

Two brief scenes are intercut at this point, which further illuminate the community's assumptions about gender roles and the division of labour, and which turn on that most traditional of female duties, the preparation of food. Three of the older women of the town carefully and proudly carry the cake they have made to the hall where the wedding reception is to take place that evening, to be warmly congratulated on their efforts by the men already there. Simultaneously, Nick's girlfriend Linda (Meryl Streep) is punched by her drunken father when she brings him his breakfast. In fact, a similar attack occurs at the reception when Stan, angered that his girlfriend is flirting with another man, ignores the man but knocks her to the floor. Clairton is thus quickly depicted as a place where unprovoked male violence against women is routine, unremarkable, and goes unpunished.

The cut back to the bar, now empty apart from the six friends, begins with the instrumental introduction to Frankie Valli's Can't Take My Eyes Off You *which, although never explicitly revealed, is assumed to be playing on the jukebox. The fact that the track was a hit single in the United States in the summer of 1967 allows us to make fairly accurate judgements about the film's time frame which point to its cultural, as well as its musical, significance. By ignoring the psychedelic, drug-related and politically inspired music that had articulated the growing domestic hostility to American involvement in Vietnam from 1967's 'Summer of Love' onward (Jefferson Airplane, the Grateful Dead, Big Brother & the Holding Company, the Doors, Country Joe & the Fish) the men effectively distance themselves from radical or subversive undercurrents. Moreover, Valli was the lead vocalist of the Four Seasons, the Italian-American group whose smart suits, neat haircuts and four-piece harmonies had given them a string of hit singles since 1962, despite the impact of the 'British Invasion' that had effectively replaced many domestic entertainers by introducing American audiences to groups like the Beatles, the Rolling Stones, and the Animals. His presence via the jukebox thus exemplifies those sentiments of insularity, continuity, and resistance to change that run through Clairton itself.*

As the vocal begins - 'You're just too good to be true' - Michael, Nick, Axel and John are at the pool table. Immediately, the flamboyant and attractive Nick emerges as the focal point of the camera; his supple and joyful dancing (Walken had trained as a dancer) contrasts with the disciplined, introspective Michael's determination to play a winning shot. The lengthy gaze he directs at Nick coincides with the line 'At long last love has arrived' - the first clue to the implied male desire that Michael has for his friend. This theme, central to so much of what follows, is repeatedly explored via asides, glances and fragments of conversation: Michael confiding to Nick during the preparations for the hunting expedition that '...without you, I'd hunt alone'; his obvious unease when Nick is visited by Linda in the trailer the two men share; the evident pleasure he shows when looking at a blow-up photograph of the young, classically beautiful Nick at the wedding reception; his sprawling naked in the street in front of Nick after his flight from the reception; the twice-repeated declaration when they finally meet in Saigon - 'Nicky, I love you'. Gledhill's observation that '(the) stag night is used less to tell Steven's heterosexual story than to set going undercurrents of unexpressed male desire between Mike and Nick' (1995, p. 80) is quite correct.

Meanwhile, Stan and Steven are seated together at the bar. While Stan freely joins in with the lyrics - 'you'd be like heaven to touch, I want to hold you so much' - Steven's reluctance to sing portrays his discomfort about his forthcoming marriage. He is tense, awkward and unsmiling, and when Stan removes his beer, simply reaches for another glass.

As the song builds towards its chorus, Nick is dancing with even greater sensuality. The watching, somewhat uneasy Michael applauds - whether at Nick's pool shot or his dancing is uncertain. Both at the pool table and the bar, there is a clear sense that the men are preparing for the climactic moment of the chorus - conversation ceases, Michael drums his cue on the floor, Nick's singing becomes louder. The moment of release in which all the men participate, 'I love you, baby!' is almost orgasmic in the release of tension and energy it brings. When the other five friends come together at the bar to continue their enthusiastic singing, Michael remains alone at the pool table, thus re-stating his position as a man apart - the acknowledged leader of the group, but an uncomfortable member in the group.

The celebration of perennial values and the mundane nature of many of the activities in the lengthy Clairton/wedding segment of The Deer Hunter are deliberately emphasised by Cimino in order to contrast all the more powerfully the waiting horrors of Vietnam. Hellmann has recognised that in this sense, 'Vietnam functions in the film as a mirror image of America, a dark landscape turning upside down the benign landscape of Cimino's mythic Alleghenies' (1991, p. 62). What is less recognised is that the character of Nick functions as a mirror image of Michael - the blonde, androgynous and extrovert Nick, who is happiest in the company of friends, against the bearded, watchful and lonely Michael, who prefers the challenges of the wilderness. It is here in the bar, during the song, that these contrasts are first illustrated; while both join in the song, the exuberance of one is juxtaposed against the caution of the other.

At this moment, the men's revelries are interrupted by the arrival of Steven's mother (Shirley Stoler). While the song continues she enters the bar, just after John has drunkenly kissed her son on the cheek. In a stereotypically comedic sequence, she drags the complaining Steven outside, much to the amusement of the others, whom she dismisses as 'bums'. However, her intervention does not threaten, but rather strengthens the unity of the group, as is shown by their spontaneous singing to her, in time with the music, of the line 'I want to hold you so much', and their collapse into laughter as Stan falls off the bar stool. The music fades as the men follow the pair outside into the street where Steven's admonition (from his mother) and teasing (from his friends) continue.

[67]

The song thus functions as a vehicle through which group cohesion can be ritually maintained in the face of potential and serious invasions - their departure from the factory, their imminent transfer to Vietnam, the marriage of one of the group, the hostility of Steven's mother. It has been suggested that 'Cimino is in love with ritual and turns every experience into an elaborate ceremony' (Quart & Auster 1980: 122). And, in fact, in his subsequent film, Heaven's Gate (1980), he chooses to exploit the ritual of the dance (with all its physical, social and cultural implications) to provide its central motif.

Participation in song is, of course, an especially potent ritual for reaffirming membership and unity, as the political importance attached to the existence of national anthems shows only too clearly. Indeed, the men engage in communal singing again, in Michael's car on the way to the hunt, and on the return to John's bar with the slain deer. In his analysis of religion, first published in 1912, Durkheim pointed to the general significance that such regular ceremonial and ritual activities have for the consolidation of the 'collective conscience' or solidarity possessed by a group, especially at times of crisis or transition:

The only way of renewing collective representations... is to retemper them... in assembled groups... Men are more confident because they feel themselves stronger; and they really are stronger, because forces which were languishing are now re-awakened in the consciousness.

(1965, p. 387)

Furthermore, when these rituals are 'performed in a state of confidence, joy, and enthusiasm' (1965, p. 389), as by the men assembled in John's bar, their regenerative capacities increase visibly. The point is compellingly made during the wedding reception, when the resident band's version of Can't Take My Eyes Off You *elicits no response from the friends, who continue to talk and laugh over the music, despite their earlier uninhibited performance of it. In this respect, the song itself is relatively unimportant - its significance lies in the properties it acquires when sung by the group, all of whom (with the exception of Steven) appear to have no family, and for whom therefore the motivation for repeated ritual acts of male bonding is that much more urgent.*

The full significance of the location of the song is revealed in two separate scenes in the third section of the film. First, when Michael and Nick finally come face to face in Saigon, it is in another bar. It too is an all-male environment, but here the entertainment is not provided by a jukebox, television and pool table, but by games of Russian roulette. Singing is replaced by screaming; camaraderie by competition; jokes by threats; generosity by greed. It has been argued that 'the two locations...dominate and epitomize the two worlds of the film' (Wood, 1986, pp. 288-289). The symbolic opposition between the security and reassurance of the bar-room rituals in Clairton and the random and chaotic reality of those in Saigon supplies the architecture around which all of the film's major events revolve.

Secondly, the film's closing scene reunites all the main characters in John's bar after Nick's funeral and, for the first time, women have also been invited - Steven's wife, Angela (Rutanya Alda) and Linda. Bewildered and uncertain, men and women search for things to do - setting the table, making the coffee, pouring the drinks. In contrast to the buoyant and confident excitement of the early scene, there is nervousness and confusion. In what has become one of the most debated film endings in recent years, they seek refuge in one final ritual. Unable to cook the eggs, the weeping John begins to sing God Bless America; *tentatively and quietly, the others, seated around the table, join in, raising their glasses at its conclusion to toast Nick. The scene has been interpreted in different ways. Hellmann believes that it is 'asserting the continuing value of the ideal embodied in a simple love for America' (1991, p. 66), whereas Wood concludes that 'if the song affirms anything, it is something already perceived as lost' (1986, p. 289). Either way, the comparison between the group's rendition of this song and* Can't Take My Eyes Off You *signals the profound shifts within the country itself, pre-Vietnam and post-Vietnam. It reveals unequivocally that* The Deer Hunter *is not a film about Vietnam; it is a film about America.*

Of course, The Deer Hunter *is not the only film to have explored the capacity of musical participation to enhance group solidarity. The singing of 'La Marseillaise' in Rick's Bar in* Casablanca *(Michael Curtiz, 1942), the defiant whistling of the* Colonel Bogey March *by the prisoners of war in* The Bridge On The River Kwai *(David Lean, 1957), the mutual performance of* My Rifle, My Pony And Me *by the besieged lawmen in* Rio Bravo *(Howard Hawks, 1959) and the drunken version of* Show Me The Way To Go Home *by the three apprehensive shark-hunters in* Jaws *(Steven Spielberg, 1975) are just a few among many instances of music's ability to create or maintain a sense of unity.*

What makes the example of Can't Take My Eyes Off You *so memorable has less to do with the song itself and more to do with the position it occupies within the film and its musical soundtrack. Its early introduction (less than ten minutes into the film) quickly and effectively substantiates the strength of the group identity that is so essential to much of what is to be revealed over the next three hours. And the familiarity of the song (a recent hit single) and the setting (a bar) help to ensure a perception of that identity as natural and uncontrived.*

In addition, The Deer Hunter *is a film of extraordinary musical, as well as visual, variety. While it may be best remembered for its theme tune -* Cavatina, *composed by Stanley Myers and performed on guitar by John Williams - it contains an unusually diverse assortment of diegetic music. John plays a Chopin nocturne on the piano in his bar; the public address system in the bowling alley plays a country duet; choral music is performed in the church at the wedding; the guests dance to Russian folk music at the reception; in the bars of Saigon, the girl dancers move to the rhythms of soul; the group's final action together in the film is to sing a hymn.* Can't Take My Eyes Off You *is notable as the single example of a contemporary pop song in the film; and its structure, building gradually and forcefully to the explosive crescendo supplied by the chorus, anticipates the construction of events within the narrative itself.*

[69]

References

Adair, Gilbert. *Hollywood's Vietnam*. New York: Proteus, 1981.

Auster, Albert & Leonard Quart. *How The War Was Remembered*. New York: Praeger, 1988.

Durkheim, Emile. *The Elementary Forms Of The Religious Life*. New York: Free Press, 1965.

Gledhill, Christine (1995) 'Women Reading Men' in Pat Kirkham & Janet Thumim, (Eds.) *Me Jane: Masculinity, Movies And Women*. London: Lawrence & Wishart, pp. 73-93.

Hellmann, John (1991) 'Vietnam And The Hollywood Genre Film' in Michael Anderegg, (Ed.) *Inventing Vietnam*. Philadelphia: Temple University Press.

Quart, Leonard & Albert Auster. (1980) *American Film And Society Since 1945*. London: Macmillan.

Wood, Robin. (1986), *Hollywood From Vietnam To Reagan*. New York: Columbia University Press,.

Fluid Figures: How To See Ghost[s] *Steve Lannin*

Unchained Melody [Righteous Brothers, 1965] / Ghost [Jerry Zucker, 1990]

Fluid Figures: How to see Ghost[s]

Steve Lannin

> I've tried to make work that any viewer, no matter where they came from, would have to respond to, would have to say that on some level 'Yes, I like it.' If they couldn't do that, it would only be because they had been told they were not supposed to like it.

(Koons, 1992, p. 112)

Ghost[1] has been labelled by critics 'The movie with ESP - Extra Silly Premise' (McIlheney, 1990, p. 73); been praised as a triumphant commercial success (Smith, 1998, p. 220) and also considered an 'under-estimated' 'generic hybrid' (1998, p. 25) by Fowkes who views comedy ghost films generally as a positive format which 'invite fluid identifications across gender stereotypes' (ibid., p. 161). With reference to gestalt psychology and narrative/metaphoric shapes that underpin Ghost's structure I shall identify other factors that have contributed to its mysterious popularity with both sexes, why the critics failed to see its potential and explain how Unchained Melody is key to a superior cultural artifact. This essay will reveal Ghost as a complex fantasy that facilitates polarised readings and can dialectically avow individualism above partnership, while simultaneously indicating the reverse.

Dead Popular

Written by H. Zaret & A. North for a long forgotten Hollywood movie, Unchained (1955), hence Unchained Melody, the song was initially a big hit in the US with an instrumental version by Les Baxter. It reached No. 1 and sold more than a million copies in the same year as the film's release. The original movie version, by black, blind singer Al Hibbler reached No. 3 and only fifth place at the Academy Awards for the Best Song category. In the UK, Jimmy Young took the song to No. 1 that same year.

Other versions were recorded, but in 1965 the Righteous Brothers revived the song, originally as a B-side, this was flipped by radio stations and reached No. 4, lasting twelve weeks on the US chart. It is considered, by many, as the definitive version. 'Unchained Melody' had some chart success for the Righteous Brothers at the time of Ghost but in Britain has since been revived far more successfully, on two occasions, both through connection to popular TV shows. Indeed, it appears to be a song that will not die.

In Music & Consumer Behaviour (1997, pp. 280-1) North & Hargreaves review research into the 'typical "product life cycle" of successful pop singles.' The results suggest, both a normal 'commercial life' for songs of 'approximately eleven weeks' (ibid., p. 281) and a clear relationship between plugging and record success. Adorno (1976) in his tirade against the popular music industry suggested there were '"evergreens" (ibid., p. 35), hits that seem to defy aging and to outlast fashions'. Unchained Melody certainly fills this criteria.

With these facts in mind it is possible to compare Sam (Patrick Swayze) the Ghost, living beyond his screen death and Unchained Melody, refusing to inhabit a normal 'commercial lifecycle', itself a 'ghost' from a previous film, and a previous era. This analogy can be extended when considering the 'invisibility' of audio media, and how in sonic form, a song can pass through walls, 'haunting' a location much in the same way Sam haunts Molly (Demi Moore) and Oda Mae (Whoopi Goldberg) during Ghost. Transposed states of existence recur as a theme throughout the film and the song's relationship to Sam's transitions is metaphoric.

Shapes in the Machine

The flesh and blood of a tone depends from the start upon its role in the melody.

(Wertheimer, 1924, p. 5)

Gestalt psychologists attempt to explain how our visual systems connect groups of visual stimuli into an overall form. This relates, as in the quote above, to how we hear a melody as one article, and not a discreet series of notes, and indeed how we are able to see a melody on a page of notation, grouping events over time and space into a simpler 'shape' or concept and enabling comparison.

Unchained Melody is embedded into the structure of Ghost and unlike other songs in compiled sound tracks is similar to a minor character, appearing on three separate occasions. Smith (1998, p. 219) describes these appearances as the film's 'most emotionally involving material'. For this reason it is useful to consider how 'melody' interacts with other elements (characters, editing, narrative) across the entire surface of the film.

Here is a compiled list of elements that could be mapped to define aspects of a film's shape and compared against inter-textual items, like the pop song:

- Over-riding visual character of it's static 'misè-en-scene' compositions and 'realist elements'.

- Visual mechanics - complex camera movements, montage, editing, and any 'formative'production aspect;

- Genre - the temporal structure as a shape - with or without comparison to similar genre;

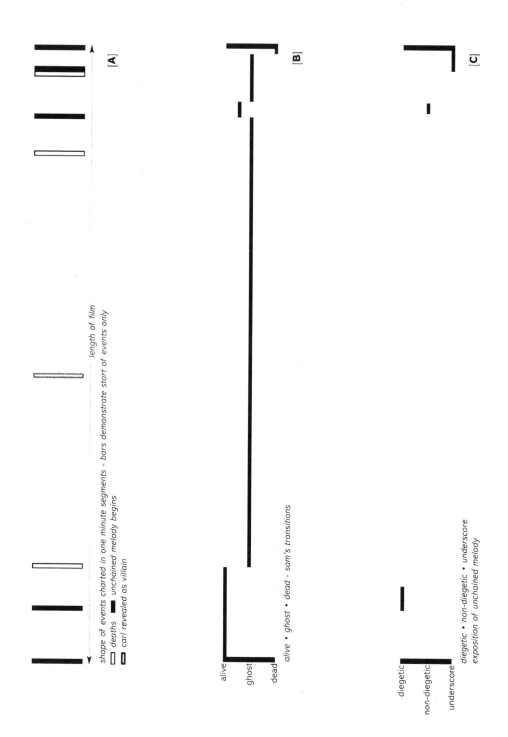

[A]

shape of events charted in one minute segments - bars demonstrate start of events only

□ deaths   ■ unchained melody begins
▨ carl revealed as villain

length of film

[B]

alive • ghost • dead - sam's transitions

alive
ghost
dead

[C]

diegetic • non-diegetic • underscore
exposition of unchained melody

diegetic
non-diegetic
underscore

- *Overall arc of the narrative and the narratives impact on our psychological drives;*

- *The gender of the genre - not just a binary choice of films for boys or girls - are the elements consistent with a particular gender of audience;*

- *Traces of the soundtrack, character dependent or scene specific, through-composed or compiled, diegetic or otherwise;*

- *Trait transitions of individual characters good to bad, masculine traits to feminine, etc. with diegetic and non-diegetic perspectives;*

- *The shape of the character inter-relations;*

- *Passive and active participants in the visual and on the soundtrack;*

- *Conceptual support structures - how audio-visual elements combine to support a metaphor or theme.*

(This list is by no means prescriptive or exhaustive)

[76]

To contemplate how an audio cultural artefact (the pop song) impacts on an audio-visual form (the movie), it is perhaps useful to visualise the two in a similar manner. Music, of course, can be notated conveniently and although there is no formalised language to document the lines and shapes of a film's conceptual transitions[2], it is not difficult to devise a process to extract individual elements and observe the shapes they form across a temporal space. (See [A])

Outlines of Transition

Ghost films engage in a fantasy of a return to pre-oedipal oneness through a masochistic fantasy, which permits a change of position.

(Fowkes, 1998, p. 123)

The device of the ghost is indeed an ideal vehicle for staging fantasies of gender flux in the context of a culture that operates along binary gender lines.

(ibid., p. 151)

An important way to appreciate how Unchained Melody *supports many of the narrative imperatives is to see how it is placed in the film as a whole, how it's shape supports the structure of transitions that activate the psychological imperatives. In diagrams (C) exposition of* Unchained Melody *and (B) - Sam's transitions, notice how Sam's transition from alive to dead mirrors the diegesis of* Unchained Melody *- whose visual exposition clarifies its diegetic nature completely in the first sequence where Sam is very much alive, in the second it is obviously non-diegetic as a ghostly Sam re-lives his physical relationship to Molly via Oda Mae and its submission into the underscore comes just before Sam's transfer to 'a better place'.*

Fowkes book (1998) which focuses heavily on Ghost, *refers to Sam's transitions as feminising, i.e. Sam is castrated in death, and made ineffectual, but she does not refer to how* Unchained Melody's *transition from diegetic, to non-diegetic, and into the underscore support this. Kassabian (2001) might contend that song placement implies the feminine, when presented, as it is, next to an orchestral score, that has traditionally, and mostly, been the preserve of male composers. So Sam's association with the pop song[3], as he and* Unchained Melody *transpose metaphysically and, the latter, diegetically at similar moments, signal his feminisation/castration.*

Further to this, characters in the film appear in transition throughout, with Oda Mae in particular transforming, separately in the perspectives of individual characters (D). Specifically her transitions include enemy/stranger to good friend, female to male and back - twice, from poor to rich and back, from fake to real, and from thief to philanthropist. See Diagrams (D, E and F).

[77]

In this instance the transitions of the soundtrack becomes a metaphor for transition generally - but not just transition from one binary opposite to another, as Fowkes (1998, p. 151) proposes, but with the possibility of different levels of existence, and differing perspectives.

Constructing Moralities

Transitions are also coded into moral/amoral(4) signifiers that weave through the film and help define its shape. A significant part of this code centres on the most famous and most parodied sequence from the film where Molly is potting at her wheel, listening to the jukebox. As Unchained Melody *begins to play she is joined by Sam, who attempts to help her pot, they then abandon this to 'make love' until the song ends.*

Breaking down this scene it is possible to discern two distinct and contradictory positions from which the sequence can be viewed. Firstly that the action is about Sam and Molly cementing their romantic partnership as a couple, and conversely/simultaneously the signs indicate we are voyeurs watching amoral sex.

The ceramics that Molly (an old fashioned sounding name) produces are not considered cutting edge fine art practice (see Koons) - the works would not offend any general public - and equally they imply someone immersed in a tradition with a conservative reputation (in art terms) - all these factors are supported by the songs on the juke box including Unchained Melody in its 'sixties' rendition. An old song, playing on outdated technology, all alluding to old-fashioned values.

Marriage is also alluded to as the song can be seen to represent three of the four traditional wedding tokens: something old - recorded in the 1960s, something borrowed - from a previous film Unchained 1955 and something blue - its lyric gives sad testimony to a distant love. Other elements of the scene support this, like the white shirt that Molly wears to pot in - unusual for a process that necessitates mess and equally symbolic of marriage and purity. The purity of their union is extended as the couple make love with clean hands across naked flesh, despite no shots of either of them washing. These visual signs are formalised in the dialogue, when Molly asks Sam to marry her a couple of scenes later.

As Molly represents the art world so Sam represents the world of business and finance, clearly defined as a confident banker in an earlier scene. The record is a product that bridges the world of art with that of commerce. Chart hits are the most conspicuous display of arts alliance with business in western culture. Unchained Melody is a signifier of their union - and having sustained its popularity for so long, might indicate a long partnership to those that remember it, (were the lyrics not also foreshadowing Sam's fate). The visual edits clarify this partnership - the song begins with a shot of Molly creating pots in her work space, establishes the mood for their union and ends as the shot cuts to the building of the bank Sam works for.

However, considering the details of the scene carefully an opposed reading emerges. The edited juxtaposition just previously discussed could indicate sex as a commercial activity (Molly's workplace-sex-Sam's workplace). Murch's editing enhances this reading, as we view the record being taken to and from the turntable, bookending the scene to suggest a mechanical process/transaction has occurred, rather than a 'romantic partnership'. The record in itself being a commercial product. In virtually all scenes the couple are joined by a third, another, who contributes to their relationship(5). During this scene the other is the song and this is how we, the audience, are implicated as voyeurs. Kassabian (2001, p. 81) in a discussion about Thelma and Louise suggested that - 'By using popular music the film grounds the entire narrative in the everyday.'(6) By using a familiar song with pan-generational appeal it is possible to withdraw from specific character identifications and engage with the sequence as an 'everyday' pornographic interlude rather than a romantic exchange, i.e. by identifying with the remembered song rather than the characters. The song's lyrics lend itself to this by being remote from the location of their affection, lines like 'I hunger for your touch' and 'I need your love, I need your love' speak for a dislocated audience, distant from the tactile experience they witness.

The 'Other', 'Oneness' and the Individual

Since the subject is necessarily divided through language, the goal of romantic union would seem to spell the end, or death of the subject. How can films reconcile the fulfilment of a desire that leads to the annihilation of the subject who originally desired it?

(Fowkes, 1998, p. 106)

Ghost *is a film about individuals. It may appear to concern romantic union but as the film ends every character we have encountered leaves the screen without a partner. Individualism is signified in one of two categories. Firstly there is 'the other', the individual who is not part of the romantic union and, in Lancanian terms, is everything that is not the subject (in a proposition that a romantic union can represent one subject for the purposes of romantic drama). Secondly there is the individual within the union, and this is expressed by methods of delaying or preventing a concluded romantic union and oppositely in the abandoned/isolated individual.*

'Other' characters are played by the two supporting actors Carl and Oda Mae - during a series of transitions these two individuals will represent a staggering variety of 'other' roles: black, homosexual/lesbian, transgender, 'homme-fatale', villain, money launderer, con-artist, thief, criminal master-mind and murderer. Many of these can be anticipated as stereotypical 'other's that threaten a 'rich, white, heterosexual' subject in Hollywood - but in this film the 'other' is also seen as a support structure to the romantic subject in Carl's case helping to re-build Sam and Mollys' home - and significantly in Oda Mae's case helping to re-build/re-live their relationship. As such the theme of individualism is simultaneously balanced by its opposite - inter-dependence. To re-reference the transition chart, in diagram (A) the point at which Carl is revealed as the master-mind behind Sam's death, at almost half-way through the film, Oda Mae has already started the transition to become Sam and Mollys' new best friend. This is a very significant transition with regard to the film's shape as a whole. Ghost *starts with three friends, together in joy and destruction to create 'space'. It ends with three individuals together in hope having survived destruction, having overcome adversity and ready to rebuild. During the process a rich, white male has been replaced by a poor, black female.*

During the second scene in which Unchained Melody *is played, Oda Mae has agreed to allow Sam's spirit to enter her body so that he can touch Molly through Oda Mae's hands. Earlier I suggested that the song might represent the 'other' in the potting sequence, as it is one of only two in which they are completely alone. In this sequence there is a nervous tension created when Molly takes Oda Maes hands to 'feel Sam'. The songs lyric now takes on an added dimension in context, it has become the 'physical love' theme for the couple but its ambiguous lyrics and performance can be read to reference the lesbian/homosexual 'other'. Questions the song's text raises in this situation might include: What are these ambiguous 'brothers' singing about? About the same person? Do they represent Sam and Carl singing for Molly, are they rivals or do they sing toward each other? Could this be about love for a man, or as 'brothers' is this an incestuous love? Is that why they are apart, obsessed but unable to be together? The visuals of the film only hint at the two women in passionate embrace - the spectator is shown Sam and Molly, with Oda Mae extinguished from the image. (Although the suggestion of lesbianism is signified also by Goldberg's previous role in* The Color Purple*). The song's performance, with two male voices, refers to a structure of two and three, three people involved, two of which form a union. A three/two shape is also paralleled in the 6/8 rhythm of* Unchained, *that is counted as two beats of three for each bar.*

> **If the goal of romance is the 'oneness' of the couple, the goal of the romantic comedy is the deferment of that oneness.**

(ibid., p. 107)

Taking Fowkes statements one stage further it seems that the goals of romantic comedy and subject retention are the same. So that while society consciously offers union, the subconscious retains the ego as imperative. In social terms it can be understood with relation to commitment phobia.

[80]

Fowkes (ibid., p. 123) also writes at length about the masochistic nature of the romance in these films. In this scene particularly, where the couple are able to hold each other but without hope of permanence or a future. The sexual connotation is akin to arousal without orgasm. Like a continuous ecstasy of desire that cannot be sated.

From Sam's individual perspective, at this point in the film, we watch a man with two women happy to pleasure him. In the reality the spectator doesn't see, two women are involved in a lesbian act for his satisfaction - this is tied thematically to the amoral reading of the potting scene. By identifying with Sam, as an individual within the union, and reconsidering the 'Unchained Melody' lyric from his perspective the masochism within both appears ecstatic. The pain of the song makes sense in this reading, they are the perfect lyrics to describe the deferred union of the romantic comedy. In the overstatement of their feelings the singers (especially in their performance) appear to be enjoying this continuous desire without conclusion.

Here Unchained Melody *is Sam's achingly beautiful prison of sustained and solitary longing. Longing that the participant cannot wish to end, trapped within, masochistically repeating the exquisite agony of unquenchable desire, knowing that to conclude is to relinquish subjecthood, and embrace the death of the ego.*

Sam, in the final scene and through the very last strains of this song, played by the orchestral backing, declares his love for Molly directly for the first time in the film. He is in no position to commit himself. In many ways the words are hollow but from Molly's perspective, and for those identifying with this woman, who has had to live through all the transitions and transformations of those around her while she has remained almost unchanged, the words give her the strength to reply with a joke. This action clarifies that she is also able to move forward as an individual, away from the destruction of her partnership.

It is a powerful balancing act between the desire and cultural imperative for romantic union and the fear of relinquishing individuality to that process. One this romantic comedy cleverly resolves in favour of the individual, whilst appearing to celebrate the union. Beyond the romantic subject, the 'other' is not just the enemy but a means of inter-dependent support.

Drawing Conclusions

The problem is - you think you're real.

(Ghost on the subway, Ghost *- 1990)*

I began this essay with a quote by conceptual artist, Jeff Koons. His large, Puppy *1992, is a sculpture made from living plants and flowers. Rarely discussed in terms of what it is, (an overtly sentimental image of a dog), it is not considered to be 'cheesy' or 'smaltzy' by critics, because the artist is referencing banal images for a culture fluent with the post-modern. His statements about using banality to 'penetrate mass consciousness' and discussion of how these items 'soothe the masses for the moment; to make them feel economically secure', assure audiences about the credibility of his intention.*

[81]

Conversely, film critics judging a Hollywood product will make no allowance for the sentimental or the melodramatic, remembering, from prior experience that these are indicators of bad movies.

Thus if abc has been previously experienced, the presentation of abcde will tend on a later occasion to be experienced as abc/de.

(Gottshcaldt, 1926, p.109)

The process of criticism is built mostly on a preoccupation with the 'big' elements e.g. the script, the performance of the actors, the cinematography and sometimes the special effects. Critics might be distracted from considering the work in front of them by referencing the directors track record (Zucker's previous films were comedies), the reputations of the ensemble, etc. Smaller elements e.g. editing, the score, songs, are often overlooked as their attention is on the 'Text', not the incidental. In a recent TV programme neuro-scientist Susan Greenfield (2000) discussed the how the brain focuses: 'We're all equipped with a means of selecting the key aspects of a scene, one at a time. This attention system allows us to concentrate on one thing, while the rest of the world falls into the background. All this happens so automatically that we don't notice it.'

Gestalt (Wertheimer, 1923, p. 71) rules suggest that as we glance at scattered items forming a shape, we have a tendency to concentrate on the whole shape rather than constituent parts. If this, as an action of the mind is true visually, then it can hold for other mental actions like concept formation. The spectator, whose only job is to watch passively, may be equally annoyed by the sentimentality and vengeful melodrama (Milne, 1990, p. 296) that Ghost undoubtedly contains but has been powerfully engaged with its stronger aspects, responding to the narrative as a continuous whole rather than extracting and focusing on the disparate parts the critic is expected to discern. Both audience and critic have simplified the film but because their attention systems have been separately focused their realities are at odds.

> ...what counts is what goes on inside our heads, what happens there is completely personal. It's not so much that our visual system rebuilds the outside world, but rather that we create from scratch our own private universe, our own reality.

(Greenfield, 2000)

Fowkes (1998) has intuited some of the powerful themes that make Ghost a significant Hollywood vehicle but was unable/disinclined to unpick how aspects of the film support her readings. The 'Gestalt' of Ghost leaves an overall impression that satisfies the sub-conscious. It hides its complexity, beneath the simple shapes of romance and fantasy.

> ...a text's unity lies not in its origin but in its destination.

(Barthes, 1977, p.148)

It is the open coding of the sign paths that can be read through the film, allowing for multiple identification trajectories and meanings that enabled the films success. Susan Hayward (2000, p. 124) in her discussion of the impact of Foucault on feminist film theory could easily have been describing the theoretical formula underpinning Ghost 'There is not a 'female' or a 'male' spectator but different socio-cultural individuals all busy producing reality as the film rolls by. Age, gender, race, class, sexuality affect reception and meaning production'.

Unchained Melody is a good example of the complex sign structures and themes that support

Ghost, *and is key to several of them. E.g. meta-physical and material transition, invisibility, morality and amorality, individualism and 'oneness', premonition, castration/feminisation. The shape of this song is as fluid as the film, inviting as many readings and also, like the film, its ambiguity is hidden by its apparent simplicity.*

Being able to view the sentimentality and melodrama as a series of parts that make up just one 'gestalt' shape across the surface of Ghost's *multi-shaped experience - they, like the flowers on Koon's* Puppy, *provide a superficial coating to help 'penetrate mass consciousness'. Beneath the 'smaltz' is a soft, complex structure that bends reality to celebrate inter-dependence and independence in a relativist ontology of almost limitless transition.*

Notes

1   *It is anticipated that readers are familiar with the plot of the most successful film in the US -1990- synopsis are available via a simple web search.*

2   *A story-board being a purely visual indicator of little use in this regard.*

3   *In gestalt terms, his proximity and similarity [Wertheimer 1923:77].*

4   *In this essay I use the word moral to reference concern with the moral, with no good/bad judge-ment intended.*

[83]

5   *Be it Carl[actor Tony Goldwyn] knocking down walls or Oda Mae enabling communication.*

6   *This is also a stabilizing factor - countering the 'fantastic' elements to come.*

References

Adorno, T. (1976)*Introduction to the Sociology of Music. Continuum*, pp. 21-38.
Barthes, R. (1977) 'Death of the Author' in Barthes, R. *Image, Music, Text*. Fontana Press. Trans. Heath, S., pp. 142-148.
Bourke, K. (1990) 'That's the Spirit'. *Manchester Evening News*, 4 October.
Chion, M. (1999) *The Voice in Cinema*. Columbia University Press, 1999, trans. Claudia Gorbman.
Fowkes, K.(1998) *Giving Up the Ghost - Spirits, Ghosts and Angels in Mainstream Comedy Films.* Michigan: Wayne State University Press.
Gottshcaldt, K. (1926) 'Gestalt Factors and Repetition', in (Ed.) Ellis, W. D. *A Source Book of Gestalt Psychology*. Kegan Paul, Trench, Trauber & Co., Ltd, 1938.
Greenfield, S. (2000) *Commentary. In: Brain Story (3):The Mind's Eye*. TV, BBC2. 1 August, 2000.
Hayward, S. (2000)*Cinema Studies - The Key Concepts*. Routledge, 2000.

Kassabian, A. (2001)*Hearing Film - Tracking Identifications in Contemporary Hollywood Film Music*. New York, USA: Routledge, 2001.

Kegan Paul, (1938) *Trench*, Trauber & Co., Ltd.

Koons, J. **(1992)** *The Jeff Koons Handbook*. Thames and Hudson.

McIlheney, B. (1990) 'Back from the Dead'. *Empire*, November, pp. 72-76.

Milne, T. (1990) *Ghost. Monthly Film Bulletin*, Oct 1990 57 (681) pp. 295-296.

North, A. C. & Hargreaves, D. J. (1997) 'Music & Consumer Behaviour' in (Eds.) Hargreaves, D. J. &

North, A. C. *The Social Psychology of Music*. New York: Oxford University, pp. 268-289.

Smith, J. *Sounds of Commerce - Marketing Popular Film Music*. Columbia University Press, 1998, pp. 219-220.

Wertheimer, M. (1924) 'Gestalt Theory', in (Ed.) Ellis, W. D. *A Source Book of Gestalt Psychology*.

Wertheimer, M. (1923) 'Laws of Organisation in Perceptual Forms', in (Ed.) Ellis, W. D. *A Source Book of Gestalt Psychology*. Kegan Paul, Trench, Trauber & Co., Ltd, 1938, pp. 71-88.

Reap Just What You Sow *Miguel Mera*

Perfect Day [Lou Reed, 1973] / Trainspotting [Danny Boyle, 1996]

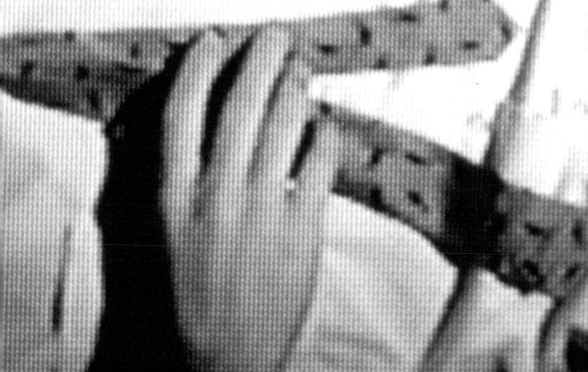

'Reap Just What You Sow': Trainspotting's Perfect Day

Miguel Mera

EXT. Park. Day

SICK BOY: *It's certainly a phenomenon in all walks of life.*

RENTON: *What do you mean?*

SICK BOY: *Well, at one point you've got it, then you lose it and it's gone forever. All walks of life: Georgie Best, for example, had it and lost it... or David Bowie or Lou Reed.*

RENTON: *Lou Reed? Some of his solo stuff's not bad.*

SICK BOY: *No, it's not bad, but it's not great either is it? And in your heart you kind of know that although it sounds all right, it's actually just shite.*

RENTON: *So who else?*

SICK BOY: *Charlie Nicholas, David Niven, Malcolm McLaren, Elvis Presley.*

RENTON: *OK, OK, OK, so what is the point you are trying to make?*

SICK BOY: *All I am trying to do Mark, is to help you understand that* The Name of the Rose *is merely a blip on an otherwise uninterrupted downward trajectory.*

RENTON: *And what about* The Untouchables?

SICK BOY: *I don't rate that at all.*

RENTON: *Despite the Academy award?*

SICK BOY: *That means fuck-all! It's a sympathy vote.*

RENTON: *So, we all get all old, we cannae hack it any more and that's it.*

SICK BOY: *Yeah.*

RENTON: *That's you're theory?*

SICK BOY: *Yeah, beautifully fucking illustrated.*

In a conventional narrative sense, the above scene from Danny Boyle's 1996 film Trainspotting does little to develop the plot, but it is comfortably accommodated within an episodic narrative structure.[1] Consequently, the scene's function could be seen as lacking a defined objective or dramatic purpose. However, one of the notable features about the sequence is the variety of cultural references made by the two characters, Sick Boy and Mark Renton. This discussion not only indicates the cultural values, interests and obsessions of the two men, providing the audience with a greater insight into their personalities, but it also introduces one of the film's significant musical figures, Lou Reed. Reed is not simply mentioned by name and his music discussed within the diegesis, but his song, Perfect Day, is subsequently heard on the film's non-diegetic soundtrack accompanying Renton as he suffers a heroin overdose. By bringing the character of Lou Reed into the foreground narrative, the filmmakers deliberately eschew one of

the fundamental concepts of film music scholarship, namely the principle of musical 'inaudibility.'
This theory, propounded by a number of writers, suggests that film music is most effective when
it works subconsciously on an audience, and that they are unaware of (and anaesthetised by) its
presence. As Gorbman states with regard to classical Hollywood practice, 'Music is not meant to
be heard consciously. As such it should subordinate itself to the dialogue, to visuals - i.e., to the
primary vehicles of the narrative' (1987, p. 73). This sense of visual hegemony with music as
the background text is reinforced by Kalinak, 'Neither easy-listening nor film music is created to
draw attention to itself, and neither demands the listener's undivided attention' (1992, p. 35).
However, the above scene does draw attention to the composer/performer of 'Perfect Day' and
by implication, the listener's attention to the music when it appears later in the film is demanded.
If it is true that 'nothing more infallibly classifies, than tastes in music' (Bourdieu, 1984, p. 18)
then the fact that Renton defends Reed's solo music immediately invites the audience to form a
link between the two men. It is this link and the use of the song Perfect Day *in* Trainspotting *that*
will be the focus for this essay.[2]

Trainspotting *is based on Irvine Welsh's novel about the drugs underground in Edinburgh, as seen*
through the eyes of Mark Renton, who is part of that world but eventually manages to distance
himself from it.[3] The film is also about friendship and loyalty, which some writers have interpreted
as being firmly rooted in the principles of 'new-laddism' (e.g. Monk).[4] Scholars have also hinted
at the film's post/anti-Thatcherite aesthetic, viewing the film in the context of the 'Cool Britannia'
re-branding of Britain undertaken by the New-Labour government (e.g. Lury).[5] As such, the film
eschews the gritty, realistic British cinema tradition of Ken Loach or Mike Leigh, for example,
opting for a stylised mise-en-scène and an intensification of the novel's black humour, to create
an alternately hilarious and harrowing narrative. Murray Smith refers to this as a 'fantasy in the
manner of magic realism' (1999, p. 225).[6] Certain critics found this stylised approach
uncomfortable, believing that it glamorised and condoned drug taking and drug culture. For
example, Shone's review in The Sunday Times *expressed grave concerns about the film's moral*
stance, claiming that Trainspotting *is a 'film about drugs that likes to say 'YES!'' (1996, p. 5).*
This viewpoint does not take into account the negative representations of drug use that
Trainspotting *also portrays, for example, Renton's overdose and Tommy's death. The director*
Danny Boyle was clearly aware of the controversy of the film's position stating that, 'If you
prolong your experience with drugs, your life will darken. The film doesn't try to hide that. But it
also doesn't try to hobble along with the consensus' (Boyle in Macnab, 1996, p. 10). Other critics
(e.g. French, Billson, Cardullo) accepted and understood this perspective, and encouraged the
film to be seen as highly moral and honest. It was perceived to be valuable in the cultural climate
of the mid-90s given the widespread use of ecstasy as a recreational drug. Stollery observes
that, 'Rather than blanket condemnation of an illegal drug use, the need for rational debate on
this issue began to be acknowledged' (2001, p. 63). The critical responses to the film therefore
indicate the moral maze that the audience is required to negotiate when viewing Trainspotting.

Not only does the music help guide the audience through this maze, but it helps place them in the mind of the main character, Mark Renton.

The Perfect Day *sequence occurs just after Renton has avoided incarceration by agreeing to enter into a rehabilitation programme in an attempt to wean himself away from heroin. The doses of methadone he is taking are simply not enough to satiate him and he visits Swanney for a 'hit' in order to help him through the day. We hear the gentle opening strains of* Perfect Day *after Renton has injected himself and falls backwards, literally sinking into the floor until he is lying in a coffin-shaped and coffin-sized pit, lined by the red carpet. Swanney realises that Renton is overdosing and drags him down the stairs onto the street. An ambulance approaches rapidly but it speeds past the two men without stopping. A taxi arrives and Swanney puts Renton in the back seat with a ten-pound note in his shirt pocket. The taxi driver takes Renton to the hospital where two hospital porters carry him inside. On a trolley Renton is rushed through the Accident and Emergency department to a doctor. The doctor tries to wake him and then gives Renton an intravenous injection that suddenly draws him from his semi-conscious state. Looking foolish, Renton sits between his parents in the back seat of a taxi as they go back home. His father carries Renton to bed.*

[88]

Aside from the harmonic, timbral and lyrical content of Perfect Day, *and its synergetic relationship with the images there are a number of extramusical factors that may have been influential in the selection of this song for the overdose scene. Throughout the first part of his career (mid 60s-70s), Lou Reed was well known as both a reporter and supporter of drug use. For example, the sybaritic lyrics of the Velvet Underground song* Heroin *(I don't know where I'm going/But I'm gonna try for the kingdom if I can/'Cause it makes me feel like I'm a man) indicate Reed's obsession with substance abuse.[7] Indeed, Lou Reed is one of few artists who genuinely led the sex-drugs-rock 'n' roll lifestyle and many of his early songs were written under the influence of alcohol or drugs, or both. This would not be significant except for the fact that Reed's drug use and abuse was not only part of his private life, but also part of his performance, such that the two became indistinguishable.*

> Onstage, he produced a syringe, pumped up a vein and proceeded to inject himself with drugs - or not - as it was difficult to see from the stalls. Either way, it didn't really matter. Reed could scarcely tell the difference himself: observers noted that he stumbled incoherently across the stage, while in private he alternated between dark periods of silence and the incessant babbling of a mind beyond control.

(Doggett, 1992, p. 2)

Song Structure

Narrative Action

(2 bar introduction)

Renton sinks into the floor until he is lying in a coffin-shaped and coffin-sized pit, lined by the red carpeted floor.

Verse 1

Just a perfect day,
Drink sangria in the park,
And then later when it gets dark,
We go home.
Just a perfect day,
Feed animals in the zoo,
Then later a movie too,
And then home.

Medium Close-up of Renton as he overdoses.

Swanney stands over him: 'Perhaps sir would like me to call for a taxi?'
Shots of ambulance rapidly approaching.
Swanney drags Renton down the stairs.

Chorus

Oh it's such a perfect day,
I'm glad I spent it with you,
Oh such a perfect day,
You just keep me hanging on.
You just keep me hanging on.

Ambulance speeds by without stopping. Renton lies in the middle of the road, Swanney sits on the pavement. A taxi arrives and Swanney drags Renton across the street towards it

Verse 2

Just a perfect day,
Problems all left alone,
Weekenders on our own,
It's such fun.
Just a perfect day,
You made me forget myself,
I thought I was someone else,
Someone good.

Swanney drags Renton into the taxi and then...

[89]

puts a ten-pound note into Renton's shirt pocket.

Shots of Renton lying in the back of the taxi.

Chorus

Oh it's such a perfect day,
I'm glad I spent it with you,
Oh such a perfect day,
You just keep me hanging on.
You just keep me hanging on.

Arrival at the hospital Accident & Emergency department. Taxi driver drags Renton out of the car onto the floor and takes the ten-pound note.

Instrumental

Two hospital porters lift Renton by his arms and ankles. On a trolley Renton is rushed to a doctor.

Coda

You're going to reap just what you sow.
(4 times)

The doctor slaps Renton on the face: 'Open your eyes, Wake up, Come on Wake up!'
Renton is given an intravenous injection and comes out of his overdose.
Mother and Father sit either side of Renton as they return home in a taxi.
Father carries Renton to his bed.

(Fig. 1) 'Perfect Day' Narrative Structure

In the early 1980s Reed began a journey to overcome his addictive tendencies by joining both Alcoholics and Narcotics Anonymous. Songs such as The Last Shot *and* Bottoming Out *chronicle his struggles at this time. Reed is, therefore, an artist whose life and work were clearly affected by drug abuse, but who overcame his addiction in order to continue writing successful music. As Stollery indicates, this suggests 'a will to live and clean up as well as celebrating the pleasures and degradations of drug use' (2001, p. 36). Reed is, therefore, both a powerful drugs/music icon, as well as a potential symbol of hope for a character such as Renton. It should come as no surprise, given the linking of their two personalities evidenced by the park scene, that Renton is the only character in the film who seriously attempts to overcome his addiction (e.g. two significant 'cold-turkey' scenes) followed by a strong indication that he will, at least temporarily, become 'clean'.*

One of the most striking features about the Perfect Day *sequence is the structural alliance of the music and images (see Fig. 1). According to* Trainspotting's *producer, 'It was the editor [Mashahiro Kirakubo] who put that music there and cut the images to it. He's the one with the real ear.' (Macdonald in Macnab, 1996, p. 10). Consequently, it is clear that there are deliberate moments of audio-visual correspondence, not least the number of edits that take place on strong musical beats and the segmentation and definition of various narrative, geographical locations according to the musical structure. For example, the first chorus coincides with the first shot of Renton lying in the street outside Swanney's flat, and the second chorus coincides with Renton's arrival at the hospital. The instrumental section coincides with the two hospital porters rushing Renton to a doctor, and the moralistic coda 'You're going to reap just what you sow' coincides with the doctor trying to wake Renton up, and so on. Given the obvious dramatic power of this sequence, it is difficult to agree with Kalinak's observations about the use of popular music in film:*

[90]

> ...the pop score's insistence on the integrity and marketability of the nondiegetic song frequently brought it into conflict with some of the basic principles of the classical model. Unlike earlier innovations which added new idiomatic possibilities, like jazz, or demonstrated the adaptability of the leitmotif, like the theme score, the pop score often ignored structural principles at the center of the classical score: musical illustration of narrative content, especially the direct synchronization between music and narrative action; music as a form of structural unity; and music as an inaudible component of the drama.

(1992, p. 187)

The problem with this circular argument is that Kalinak assumes that the 'classical model' she highlights is the only model, as if the 'basic principles' she defines are somehow a law applicable to all film music. Kalinak's view does not account for different audience perceptions with regard to film music's style, purpose and form. Clearly, Perfect Day *is the form of this sequence and glues the various images together, performing exactly the same function as many especially composed scores which gravitate 'toward moments when continuity is most tenuous, to points of structural linkages on which the narrative chain depends' (Kalinak, 1992, p. 80). The music is closely synchronised to the narrative content, because the narrative content has, in fact, been shaped around the music, or as Murray Smith states 'the film appropriates the whole song, drawing out and exploiting all of its emotional colours' (2002, p. 68). The song is certainly not an 'inaudible' component of the drama, but why should it need to be? Film music scholars seem to have grave concerns about what Bob Last describes as* MTV Moments *(in Wootton, & Romney, 1995, p. 186), that is the sudden appearance of pop video in the middle of a film. However, critics do not complain about the use of Puccini's aria* Chi il bel sogno di Doretta *(from La Rondine) in the film* A Room with A View *(Ivory, 1986). Perhaps this is because the Italian words are less 'visible' to the mainly English speaking audience. It could of course be argued that the music in* Trainspotting *would be less visible to a non-English speaking audience or that Italian 'pop' songs would be more suitable for English language films. However, I suspect that the* Room with a View *example merely highlights a critical hierarchy defined by musical style not content. There are plenty of examples where film music sheds its invisibility in order to make dramatically potent statements, for example, the shower sequence in* Psycho *(Hitchcock, 1960), the use of Mahler in* Death in Venice *(Visconti, 1971), or the battle sequence in Kurosawa's* Ran *(1985). Kalinak's concern about the preciseness and effectiveness of the musical illustration of narrative content, however, needs further investigation. Without detailed examinations of the use of pop music within film which reveal the artistic choices and dramatic effects of the music, critics will continue to argue that, 'It is a debatable point whether these films and similar types have been 'scored' in the strictest sense of the word. Any one of a thousand songs could serve the identical purpose' (Bazelon, 1975, p. 30).*

[91]

A number of writers have commented on the ironic nature of the Perfect Day *sequence. Street, for example, suggests that the song's 'languid tones and lyrics' (2000a, p. 187) initially represent Renton's release of tension and supposed feelings of serenity.8 However, as the narrative progresses we become aware that the song becomes 'completely ironic as what started out as a scene in which Renton's desperation, depression and loneliness is 'cured' by heroin, ends up as a nightmare of near-death, anything but a perfect day' (Street, 2000a, p. 187). Clearly, understanding how this irony is achieved is the key to understanding the use of* Perfect Day *within the overdose sequence. The observation about the 'languid tones and lyrics' begins to provide some of this information, but does not go nearly far enough, and writers such as Petrie simply state that the use of the song is ironic without providing any further insights (2000, p. 196). Stollery, on the other hand, specifies some of the particular music/image features that help to make the sequence so effective, claiming that the music 'adds meaning and significance to the film, and the film in turn added new meaning and significance to the music.'*

It epitomises the film's stance on drug taking. Renton reaps both the pleasure and pain as this soothing piece of music plays on the soundtrack over images of him close to death.

(Stollery, 2001, p. 37)

The suggestion that both music and picture are changed by each other in this combination and consequently provide a new, unified, moralistic meaning for the sequence indicates a strong synergetic film/music relationship. This is a concept contradicting what Cook describes as the 'terminological impoverishment epitomized by film criticism's traditional categorization of all music-picture relationships as either parallel or contrapuntal' (1998, p. 107). Furthermore, the fact that the sequence's synergy is viewed in the context of a simultaneous representation of pleasure and pain provides a valuable insight into why this particular song is used and how it closely illustrates narrative content in order to achieve its intended powerful commentary. It is not simply the song's combination with the sequence's harrowing images that creates irony, but more that the song itself already has contradictory qualities that make it particularly suited for use in this context. As critic Ellen Willis enigmatically states, referring to the album from which Perfect Day *was taken, 'Transformer is easy (sic) to take as medicine that tastes like honey and kicks you in the throat. Take a song like* Perfect Day. *A lovely, soft ode to an idyll in the park... or is it?' (Bockris, p. 211). On first inspection, therefore, the song's lyrics would seem to revel in a hedonistic pursuit of happiness, however phrases such as 'I thought I was someone else, someone good' or 'You're going to reap just what you sow' open up other interpretative possibilities. In addition, the meaning of the repeated line, 'You just keep me hanging on,' is ambiguous and acquires an intense and touching meaning as Renton literally tries to hang on to his life as it threatens to ebb away. However, the duality of meaning contained within the song is not just occasionally hinted at by its lyrics, but also strongly defined by its unconventional harmonic structure.*

[92]

The two-bar introduction that accompanies Renton as he sinks into the floor already provides us with some of the ambiguity vital to the pleasure/pain conception of the sequence. The opening consists of gentle piano movement lightly accompanied by a sparse use of bass and drums which lilts in 12/8 time and alternates between two chords: F major and Bb minor (ex. 1). The fact that the F major chord is the first chord that is heard suggests that the audience perceive this introduction as being in the key of F major containing an altered chord based on the fourth of the scale (i.e. Bb minor),[9] which is a common harmonic modification present in many slow pop songs.

This pattern sets-up an anticipation in the listener, who is expecting (consciously or subconsciously) an F major chord to follow. However, when the first chord of the verse appears (ex. 2) it is an unexpected repetition of a Bb minor chord encouraging the listener to re-think the introduction as a dominant (F major) tonic (Bb Minor) relationship. The simple alternation of two

(ex. 1) Perfect Day Introduction

chords, therefore, allows Reed to create a deliberately ambiguous harmonic situation from the very outset of this song. This is further compounded by the fact that the verse's harmony begins to circumnavigate the circle of fifths[10] descending from Bb minor to Gb major. This has the effect of destabilising the Bb minor tonal centre, which is only clarified when we hear the words 'when it gets dark we go home' and Eb minor (subdominant) and F major (dominant) chords bring us back to an expectation of a Bb tonal centre. The effect is that of music slowly winding out of control.

The fact that the song's chorus (Oh its such a Perfect Day, I'm glad I spent it with you), is in Bb Major, contrasting and alternating with the verses' Bb minor statement, also compounds the duality of the songs harmonic structure, creating a bitter-sweet personification of the pleasure/pain concept. Indeed, this contrast is heightened by the thickening of the texture and the increase in volume that takes place during the chorus. Reed's vocal quality also varies from reflective understatement in the verses to an impassioned desperation in the chorus, which is partly due to the 'reverberant multitracking' of his voice (Smith, 2000, p. 68). Of course, the average listener is unlikely to be consciously aware of the complexity of the song's harmonic relationships. However, I believe that they would sense something of the distinctiveness of the musical vacillation and consistent avoidance of resolution which characterises Perfect Day and makes it uniquely suitable for use in Trainspotting. As Lury suggests, the film's success depends upon 'ambiguity and its refusal to offer a consistent morality.' (2000, p. 107). Therefore, the sound of the song Perfect Day, with its contradictory musical message, closely reflects Trainspotting's moral standpoint.[11]

There are advantages and disadvantages to using both 'pop' and 'classical' music and advantages and disadvantages to using pre-existent or especially composed scores. However, the concept of the use of pop music in film as artistically bankrupt is patently wrong. The dramatic power of the Perfect Day sequence, undermines many of the negative theories which suggest that, 'Many times the songs bear little or no relation to what is on the screen' (Prendergast, 1992, p. 286) or that 'while pop records are extremely effective in suggesting a film's sense of

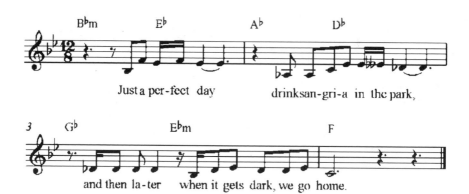

(ex. 2) Perfect Day Verse

time or place, they remain somewhat limited in terms of their other dramatic functions' (Smith, J. 1998, p. 221). The Trainspotting soundtrack powerfully resonates with its audience, through a number of cultural, verbal, and musical signifiers in ways, which a traditional orchestral score would have struggled to achieve. What is clear, is that there needs to be a much more balanced approach in film music scholarship. Rather than classifying rules for music in films to follow, or suggesting particular types of music that are more worthy of study than others, film music scholars need to ask: 'is this music dramatically apt and effective, and if so why?'

Notes

[1] Stollery argues that the episodic narrative structure is influenced by European art cinema (2000, p. 23).

[2] There are, of course, a variety of other music tracks used throughout the film which fall loosely into three categories; 90s Dance Music (Leftfield, Underworld), Britpop (Elastica, Blur, Sleeper, Pulp), & Nostalgia Pop (Iggy Pop, Lou Reed, Heaven 17). Space does not permit a detailed discussion of the individual tracks, the various categories and their interaction with each other, or their filmic functions, but both Stollery (2000, pp. 34-39) and Smith (2002, pp. 65-74), provide some useful insights into the soundtrack as a whole.

[3] Irvine Welsh himself appears in the Trainspotting film as the character Mikey Forrester.

[4] New-Laddism was a response to and reaction against feminist models of masculinity. Using irony

as one of its fundamental tools, new-laddism rejects feminist criticisms and promotes archetypal male pursuits. The attitude is exemplified by the 90s 'lads' magazine, Loaded.

5 'Cool Britannia' was intended to re-focus international notions of British identity in terms of class and culture, emphasising tolerance, ethnic diversity and middle-class creative entrepreneurialism.

6 Smith expands this concept in Trainspotting (2002), pp. 75 - 83, where he discusses the film's 'black magic realism'.

7 Reed is even reported to have, on occasion, sold drugs (see Bockris, p. 47).

8 This is contextualised by the film's opening sequence where a number of characters are seen enjoying the pleasures of heroin. For example, Renton's states in voice-over 'Take the best orgasm you ever had and multiply it by a thousand and you're still nowhere near it.'

9 In F major we would normally expect the 4th chord of the scale to be Bb major.

10 The circle of fifths is the arrangement of the tonics of the 12 major or minor keys by ascending or descending perfect fifths, thus making a closed circle.

11 As a brief postlude to this analysis it is interesting to note that following the release of the film and its soundtrack albums, the BBC produced their own version of the song 'Perfect Day'. Regularly screened on BBC television during 1997 as a corporate advertisement, it was also released as a single with all profits going to Children in Need (A charity that raises money in order to support organisations that look after the physical, emotional and social needs of children in difficult circumstances). The promotional video featured a wide variety of artists including: Lou Reed, David Bowie, Joan Armatrading, Tom Jones, Heather Small, Elton John, Boyzone, the BBC Symphony Orchestra, Suzanne Vega, Courtney Pine, Lesley Garrett, Tammy Wynette and the Brodsky String Quartet among others. The purpose of this advertisement was doubtless to emphasise the idea that BBC lives up to its principle of providing a service for a diverse audience. Significantly, despite the associations of the song with the film Trainspotting, the BBC believed that 'Perfect Day' would be a suitable emblem for its corporate identity. It is clear that the 'Trainspotting phenomenon has become a cultural reference point' (Stollery, 2000, p. 37), and has brought Lou Reed's song back into the public consciousness.

References

Bazelon, I. (1975) Knowing the Score: Notes on Film Music, New York: Van Nostrand Reinhold.

Billson, A. (1996) 'They're Smart, They're Droll, They're Homegrown' *The Sunday Telegraph: Sunday Review,* 25 February, p. 11.

Bockris, V. (1995) *Lou Reed: The Biography*, London: Vintage.

Bourdieu, P. (1984)*Distinction: A Social Critique of the Judgement of Taste*, London: Routledge & Kegan Paul.

Brown, R. S. (1994) *Overtones and Undertones: Reading Film Music*, Los Angeles: University of California Press.

Cardullo, B. (1997) 'Fiction into Film, or Bringing Welsh to a Boyle' *Literature/Film Quarterly*, Vol. 25, No. 3, pp. 158-162.

Cook, N. (1998) *Analysing Musical Multimedia*, Oxford University Press.

Doggett, P. (1992) *Lou Reed: Growing Up in Public*, London: Omnibus Press.

French, P. (1996) 'Jane Spotting' *The Observer: Observer Review*, 25 February, p. 11.

Frith, S. (1983)*Sound Effects: Youth, Leisure and the Politics of Rock 'n' Roll*, London: Constable.

Frith, S. (1988) *Facing the Music*, Cambridge: Polity Press.

Gorbman, C. (1987) *Unheard Melodies: Narrative Film Music*, Indiana University Press.

Hodge, J. (2000) *Trainspotting*, London: Faber, 1999/r..

Kalinak, K. (1992) *Settling the Score: Music and the Classical Hollywood Film*, University of Wisconsin Press,.

Kemp, P. (1996)'Trainspotting' *Sight and Sound*, Vol. 6, No. 3, March p. 52.

Longhurst, B. (1995) *Popular Music and Society*, Cambridge: Polity Press.

Lury, K. (2000)'Here and Then: Space, Place and Nostalgia in British Youth Cinema of the 1990s' *British Cinema of the 90s*, Murphy, R. (Ed.), London: BFI, pp. 100-108.

Macnab, G. (1996) 'Geoffrey Macnab Talks to the Team that Made Trainspotting' *Sight and Sound*, Vol. 6, No. 2, February pp. 8-11.

McLary, S. & Walser, R. (1990) 'Start Making Sense! Musicology Wrestles with Rock', Frith S. and Goodwin, A. (Eds.), *On Record: Rock, Pop, and the Written Word*, New York: Pantheon pp. 277-292.

Middleton, R. (2000)'Popular Music Analysis and Musicology: Bridging the Gap' *Reading Pop*, Oxford University Press, pp. 104-121.

Monk, C. (2000) 'Men in the 90s' *British Cinema of the 90s*, Murphy, R. (Ed.), London: BFI, pp. 156-166.

'Underbelly UK: the 1990s underclass film, masculinity and the ideologies of 'new' *Britain' British Cinema, Past and Present*, Ashby, J. & Higson, A. (Eds.), London: Routledge, 2000b, pp. 274- 287.

Moore, A. F. (2001) *Rock: The Primary Text*, Aldershot: Ashgate, 1993/r.

O'Hagan, A. (1996)'The Boys are Back in Town' *Sight and Sound*, Vol. 6, No. 2, February pp. 6-8.

Petrie, D. (2000) *Screening Scotland*, London: BFI.

Prendergast, R. M. (1992) *Film Music: A Neglected Art*, New York: W.W. Norton.

Romney, J. & Wooton, A. (1995) (Eds.) *Celluloid Jukebox: Popular Music and the Movies Since the 50s*, London: BFI Publishing, 1995.

Self, W.(1996) 'Carry On Up the Hypodermic' *The Observer: Preview*, 11-17 February, pp. 6-9.

Shepherd, J. (1991) *Music as Social Text*, Cambridge: Polity Press.

Shone, T. (1996)'Needle March' *Sunday Times: Culture Supplement,* 25 February, p. 5.

Shuker, R. (2001)*Understanding Popular Music*, London: Routledge.

Smith, J. (1998) *The Sounds of Commerce: Marketing Popular Film Music*, New York: Columbia University Press,.

Smith, M.(1999)'Transnational Trainspotting' *The Media in Britain*, Reading, A. & Stokes, J. (Eds), London: Macmillan, pp. 219-227.

Smith, M (2002) *Trainspotting: BFI Modern Classics*, London: British Film Institute.

Stollery, M. (2001) *Trainspotting*, London: York Press.

Street, S. (2000)'Trainspotting' *European Cinema: An Introduction*, Forbes, J. & Street, S., London: Macmillan, 2000a, pp. 183-192.

Street, S. (2000) *British Cinema in Documents*, London: Routledge.

Thompson, A. O.(1996) 'Trains, Veins and Heroin Deals' *American Cinematographer*, Vol. 77, No. 8, August, pp. 80-86.

Blonde Abjection: Spectatorship & The Abject Anal Space In-Between   *Phil Powrie*

Stuck In The Middle With You [Stealers Wheel, 1973] / Reservoir Dogs [Quentin Tarantino, 1992]

Blonde Abjection: Spectatorship and the Abject Anal Space In-Between

Phil Powrie

That's a little too close to shit.

(Tarantino/Mr Brown)

The most notorious scene in Reservoir Dogs *is the severing of the cop's ear by Mr Blonde, made infamous by Mr Blonde's soft-shoe shuffle to Stealer's Wheel 1973 hit song,* Stuck in the middle with you. *The received notion of the song is that it works anempathetically, its anodine lyrics counterpointing the violence. After exploring this view, I shall show how the song also works in harmony with the image-track: what you see and what you hear may be incongruous, but they are congruent. On the other hand, I shall then argue, there is counterpoint, but it is not between what* you see *and what* you hear; *it is between the* act of hearing *and the* act of seeing. *The disarray into which the sequence throws spectatorial affect forces us to confront ourselves as spectators, in the act of spectating. We are, as the song says, 'stuck in the middle' of a sado-masochistic scenario where what you see and what you hear collide and collapse into each other in an abject space whose focus is faecalisation, a delight in smearing shit, as Sharon Willis has recently observed. Put more simply, if provocatively, the reservoir dogs turn into reservoir turds, rejected and ejected as cloacal objects, so that spectators can reaffirm their status as subjects.*

Pure Cinema or Pure Horror?

When Reservoir Dogs *was shown at Spain's Sitges horror film festival, a number of people reportedly walked out of the ear-cutting scene, including horror directors Wes Craven and Rick Baker. The latter is supposed to have said to Tarantino: 'You're dealing with real-life violence, and I can't deal with that' (Barnes & Hearn, 1999, p. 48). There were similar scenes at the Sundance Film Festival, where the walk-outs were all by women (Woods, 1998, p. 45). Harvey Weinstein of Miramax, who bought the film, tried to persuade Tarantino to cut the sequence (Peary, 1998, p. 29). Tarantino refused, and as a result, it has been suggested, the film did less well than originally expected in theatres ($3 million; see Bernard, 1995, p. 191), but sold twice as many videocassettes in the USA as would have been expected. In the UK, where video release was banned, the film did well ($6 million), and gained a cult following similar to the* Rocky Horror Picture Show *(Sharman, 1975) as was reported in London's* Evening Standard:

[100]

The Prince Charles Cinema has screened Reservoir Dogs for the past two years. Every week passionate groupies turn up wearing the wicked suits and carrying plastic guns. They have become known as the Doggies (...). Later this month the Doggies are holding a convention at which they will each receive a fake severed ear, complete with dripping 'blood'. A hundred ears will be given away as a tribute to the dedicated Doggies who have made it the cinema's most successful film.

(Quoted in Barnes & Hearn, 1996, pp. 48-49).

The cult of the ear scene alerts us to the camp nature of the violence in the film. Apologists pointed out that the tone of the film is partly comical, which underlines its unreality (rather than the 'real' violence which horrified the horror directors), and that in any case the body count in the film is less high than in many violent films. They similarly pointed out, as did Tarantino, that we do not see the ear being cut. The severed ear clearly became and has remained a fetish, in both the vulgar sense of an object which is adored by some and reviled by others, and the more psychoanalytical sense of a stand-in for the penis. I shall be exploring this latter sense below, with particular reference to the ear as an abjected 'bad object'; but first we need to resolve the apparent contradiction between those who were too horrified to watch the scene and those for whom it was acceptable camp excess.

The answer lies in the way one critic described the scene, calling it 'needlessly sadistic' (McCarthy, 2000, p. 16). The issue here is one of gratuitousness. The torture scene is excessive and serves no apparent purpose other than to be excessive within what is already an excessively violent film. Because of its excess, it serves as the focal point for that violence, a totem, or fetish, embodying meaning for some, but, because disembodied, lack of meaning for others. This binary opposition is also, at least potentially, a gender opposition. The way the film has been presented, as we saw in the reception details given above, suggests that those for whom the scene gives the film meaning are men. This is a boy's film, a geek's film, a film which takes place, as the title of a Sight and Sound article has it, in 'the men's room' (Taubin, 2000). Women have no major part to play in the film, [1] *and, apparently, cannot watch either. Tarantino's frequent assertions that the scene was not only his favourite, but also his mother's* [2] *is clearly a means of reclaiming a non-gendered spectatorial space. On the face of it, however, this is men's business, a strictly male affair, where the group of men in the film attract 'groupies', feminized men; for although the Evening Standard does not tell us whether the Doggies included women, the chances are that the majority of the Doggies, like the Reservoir Dogs themselves, were men. The lavatorial associations (men's room, business) and the feminization I have implied are important, and we shall return to them at the end of this chapter. But we still need to resolve the apparent contradiction between those who were too horrified to watch the scene - women - and those for whom it was acceptable camp excess - men - , and which I suggested is linked to gratuitousness.*

The use of the song is crucial here. It is played on K Billy's Sounds of the 70s, *a radio programme which accompanies much of the film. The programme is referred to in the pre-credits sequence where Nice Guy Eddie talks about the ballad* The Night the Lights Went out in Georgia, *and it is heard for the first time at the beginning of the credits sequence. The programme was created by Tarantino and Roger Avary, who 'wrote all the commercials (...), traffic reports, editorials, everything. We got a bunch of actors and recorded them, and that's what's playing (...). It was great fun creating your own world that way' (Ciment & Niogret, 1998, p. 21). The DJ, voiced by comedian Steven Wright, announces the songs in a comical drawl, announcing* Stuck in the Middle with You *in the following terms: 'Joe Egan and Gerry Rafferty were a duo known as Stealer's Wheel when they recorded this Dylanesque pop bubble-gum favourite from April of 1974. They reached up to number 5.'* 3 *The song is crucial because it quite literally underscores the gratuitousness of the violence. Its 'pop bubble-gum' nature jars with the violence, making it more disturbing, as Tarantino pointed out: 'It's a great ironic counterpoint to the roughness and rudeness and disturbing nature of the film to have this "What's wrong with this picture?" music playing along with it. In some ways it takes the sting off, in some ways it makes it more disturbing' (Ciment & Niogret, 1998, p. 21).*

That gratuitousness can be interpreted in two ways: a moment of pure cinema, according to Tarantino, or pure horror according to many reviewers. Both points of view have in common the view that the song, by virtue of its anodine lyrics, suggests comical incongruity, and that this somehow lulls audiences into a sense of false security, thereby increasing the shock value of Mr Blonde's sadistic act. Audiences, in this view, are saying to themselves: 'Surely he isn't really going to torture the cop; the song is far too nice for that.' The shock of being forced to witness the torture, of being forced to accept that violence has been done to audience expectation (and I stress audience, *since it is the song which seems to suggest that such violence is unthinkable), is what constitutes both pure cinema and pure horror. It is pure cinema for those (men) who can disembody their affect in the same way that the ear is disembodied, who are disaffected, and who can resolve the twin tracks of hearing and seeing in a moment of congruent incongruence: for them, the radically different makes sense. But it is pure horror for those (women) whose affect is incorporated, who identify themselves with the violence done to the objectified and helpless cop. For them, it is incongruous congruence: the radically different does not make sense, except as a manifestation of something radically different, 'maleness'. Or as Ella Taylor points out, 'the torture scene infuriates me because it has no point other than to show off its technique' (Taylor, 2000, p. 24).*

Taylor's comment, however, hints at a potential problem in the binaries which appear to structure the reception of the film. On the one hand we appear to have women (bodies) who recoil because they experience the violence as 'real' rather than constructed; on the other, men (minds), who intellectualise the violence, seeing it in terms of cinematic technique. But as we have seen, there were men who reacted from the female position, just as Taylor reacted from the male position. In other words, there may well be a binary, but it is not necessarily gendered. The response of the fan, whether male or, possibly, female, is: 'it's gross, but it's well done, isn't that cool?'; whereas the response of the spectator who walks out, whether male or female, is: 'it's gross, but it's well done, isn't that really gross?'. [4]

In both cases, the spectator's response is one of distance, a forced admiration of male narcissism, which as we shall now see, leads the spectator into a paradoxical position. We are as radically distanced from Mr Blonde as he is from the cop; they are worlds apart. He has cut off the ear to make the cop understand that he, Mr Blonde, does not have a boss. But the ear which he holds in a desperate attempt to get the cop to listen to him, cannot hear (because disembodied), and the cop cannot speak (his mouth is taped up). To pursue the dialogue which is attempting to reassert Mr Blonde's mastery, he therefore assumes the place of the cop: 'Hey, what's goin' on?' he says laughingly into the severed ear (Appendix shot 20). The question could originate either in the ear as disembodied, or the ear could be seen as somehow standing in for the cop. In the end it does not matter much, because Mr Blonde is obliged to create an interlocutor. But that interlocutor has been fragmented, and Mr Blonde desperately tries to bring the two bits - the body and the ear - together again. 'Hey, hear that?', he then says to the cop, pretending that the disembodied hole (the severed ear) is still part of a whole (the body). [5]

[103]

This is a moment of pure cinema, then, in that it radically refuses normal logic. A body disintegrates before us, and yet is still assumed to be whole. The song is bivalent in this context. In its empathetic function, it insistently reasserts that which has been lost, 'subjecthood'. This is because it is 'about' someone who is the centre of affect, surrounded by inconsistent bodies, jokers and clowns, and seems to refer, as we shall explore below, to the predicament of the cop. The song therefore keeps together the coherent singular subject-position which the visuals are trying to rend asunder, while encouraging us to identify with the cop. This is matched by the way it counters the violence we see, suggesting, as pointed out above, that what we fear (torture) cannot really happen. But this function is anempathetic - the song contrasts with what we see, at least in appearance - distancing us from the cop with whom we might well be identifying, and thus calling our subjectivity into question. In other words, the song both reinforces a singular subject-position with which we are aligned, and undermines it.

In this section, we have seen how the song manages to support two radically opposed readings: that of the film buff, who might find the sequence, like Tarantino, 'cinematically exciting' (Peary, 1998, p. 29), and that of the spectator who refuses in horrified disgust the spectacle of a dissociated, fragmented male body, collocated with the spectacle of male narcissism predicated on that dissociation. The song manages to do this because it appears to be so unrelated to what we see going on on-screen. In the next section, I shall argue that the song is in fact more closely related to what is happening on-screen than would at first appear.

Mind the Gap

There are undoubtedly points within the song which seem to parallel what we see on-screen, the most obvious being that it seems to refer to the predicament of the cop, as mentioned above. Indeed, when faced with apparent contradictions, our most likely reaction, after the first pure cinema/pure horror reaction, is that of searching for meaning so as to resolve perplexity by meaning-production, to normalise fragmentation between aural and visual signs on the one hand, and between them and our senses, into an aesthetic. 6

One of the more obvious points of contact, it has been suggested, is the moment when the words 'please...please' in the song fade in as Mr Blonde returns to the warehouse with a can of petrol, the words thus 'stressing Patrolman Nash's predicament almost unbearably' (Woods, 1998, p. 42). The fact that the subject of the song says he is scared in case he falls off his chair would seem to uphold a parallelism between him and the cop, the cop being 'stuck in the middle' with Mr Blonde, who might well be described as a 'joker' or 'clown'.

On the other hand, other parts of the song seem to suggest a parallelism between Mr Blonde and the subject of the song, since Mr Blonde seems to 'find it hard to keep this smile from (his) face', seems to be 'losing control', and to be, literally as he dances around, 'all over the place'. But such coincidences are superficial; moreover, they are not consistent with the singular subject-position upon which the approach depends if we were to push it to its logical conclusion. The impossibility of anchoring the utterances in the song in a singular, stable subject-position merely confirms what we knew from the last section, that the song leads to unstable identifications which allow radically different meanings to surface.

Nevertheless, there is congruence on a more general level rather than at the level of character and character identification. That congruence works in two ways. First, the lyrics of the song sketch out a recognizable location (a party), even if there is no recognizable narrative. They evoke a feeling of dislocation, of being out of place, much as the extreme violence of the torture scene was felt by many to be excessive, in other words out of place. In this sense then the song underscores and supports what we see because both celebrate dislocation. It might be argued that there is a difference between a party and a torture scene. Depending on the party, of course, that might be a matter of opinion, but the notion of distance between the singer and the jokers and clowns around him has its correlate in the distance Mr Blonde attempts to create between himself as Master and the cop as Slave, a distance confirmed in the severing of the ear.

There is a second, and more interesting type of congruence, closely linked to the first, even if at first sight it might seem very different. The song creates a sense of security, apparently the antithesis of the feeling of dislocation mentioned above. It does so first by its recognizable folk-rock style, and second by its structure, whose strophic nature, like most popular song, anchors us, as well as structuring the listening frame by its appeal to chains of repeated forms such as the verse/chorus. [7] *The song can be seen as an antidote to the visual, comforting us by its cyclical nature, and working against the linearity of the torture we see developing on-screen. But there is a deeper type of security too inherent in this function of the song, which is stronger than the aural as antidote to the visual. It is the rather more terrifying, if paradoxical security of the inevitable.*

This security is connected not to the rupture and surprise which the pure horror argument seems to suggest - 'He really is going to cut his ear, and I wasn't expecting that' - but to congruence and inevitability - 'I knew all along that he was going to cut his ear, but preferred to think otherwise'. The shift in emphasis I have suggested may well remind the reader of the disavowal which film theorists have placed at the heart of watching a film. Mannoni's 'I know very well, but all the same...', cited by Metz as the fundamental fetish structure of spectatorship, corresponds to our hypothetical 'I knew all along that he was going to cut his ear, but preferred to think otherwise' (Mannoni, 1969; Metz, 1982); after all, Mr Blonde tells the cop early on that he will torture him (see Appendix shot 10). There is counterpointing, and, as this reference to issues of spectatorship suggests, it goes much deeper than a superficial anempathetic relationship between soundtrack and image-track. The counterpointing is that between seeing and hearing as activities, not between the semiotic structures of different tracks.

[105]

Put more simply, the sequence forces us to confront ourselves as viewer-listeners. The shock of the severed ear is the shock of having disavowal - 'I choose to pretend that what I am seeing really exists when I know that it doesn't' - , which is predicated on the homogeneity of soundtrack and image-track, radically dislocated by destructive excess. We can visualise this in the following way:

The gap we may have felt existed between what we hear and what we see, but which arguably is insufficiently excessive to undermine disavowal (as explained above, we look for surface parallels to normalise the gap), is radicalised by the severing of the ear. One reason why the severing of the ear manages to do this is that it parallels the gap between what we see and what we hear, and so radicalises the gap by making it excessively visible through embodiment. In other words, the song is separated from what we see in the same way that the ear is separated from its body. The sequence is 'pure cinema' not just because what you see and what you hear are in opposition, but because they are at the same time parallel; they are both different and the same. The sequence is 'pure horror' because whether we identify ourselves with the cop (and this is what Tarantino thought we would do; see his comments for the filmscript in the Appendix, linked to shot 12: 'Then he reaches out and CUTS OFF the cop's/our ear') - what used to be called secondary identification, or whether we identify ourselves with the apparatus - what used to be called primary identification, and which I have labelled the activities of seeing and hearing - the end result is the same. We are dislocated, ejected from a 'safe' subject-position. The horror of the ear, then, is that it fragments a desired but illusory totality; it confirms what we already knew, that we are 'gapped'. The illusory subject-position, which is in fact composed of different but coterminous activities, is split apart into point of view (here) and point of hearing (hear), leaving a gap, a fissure, an abyss, as we struggle to instate a location, thinking, wrongly, that we are struggling to reinstate our location.

In this section, we have seen how the song works as much with as against the image-track. The analysis has been structural, and in that respect it has not addressed one of the key components

$$\frac{\text{song}}{\text{visuals}} \; \| \; \frac{\text{ear}}{\text{body}}$$

of the horror we might feel on viewing the sequence: the disgust associated with particular forms of tactility, such as dismemberment, flesh being split open, bleeding wounds; in other words, the abject. This will be the focus of the final section.

The Abject and the Anal

The abject is, according to Julia Kristeva, the pre-Œdipal and female part-object we expel in horror and disgust, but which is a necessary component of our identity (Kristeva, 1982). The abject is linked to the maternal, to lack of control and helplessness, to all the fluids we might associate with early childhood (vomit, blood, urine, excrement). The abject is a liminal state, an in-between, poised on the cusp of subject-hood, but not quite yet subjecthood. In the abject, we might ask the question 'who am I?', and the response would be 'I'm not really very sure, but I do know that I am not that' (vomit, blood, urine, excrement). The link with the maternal is key to understanding why the abject object in this film is an ear, rather then, say, a severed finger as in Bound *(Wachowski and Wachowski, 1996). Song is normally associated with the maternal, as we know from psychoanalytical accounts going back to the work of Guy Rosolato; and the visual aspect of film has been stereotypically associated with the masculine, as we saw above. We can therefore modify our above figure thus:*

The problem is that song is not only associated with the maternal but with strong women in this film. The film opens with a discussion of the 'meanings' of Madonna's Like a Virgin, *as Mr Brown/Tarantino claims that the song is about pain for the woman ('The pain is reminding a fuck machine what is was like to be a virgin'), while the more sentimental Mr Blonde claims 'It's about a girl who is very vulnerable and she's been fucked over a few times. Then she meets some guy who's really sensitive'. Later in the opening scene the group of men discusses Vicki Lawrence's hit single from 1973,* The Night the Lights Went Out in Georgia, *referring directly to the fact that the song is about a woman killing her brother's wife and lover. In a later scene (which is a flashback even further into the diegesis than the opening scene), reference is made to Teresa Graves. Graves, a singer associated with producer Don Kirschner in the late 1960s, was the first black actress to have her own TV show,* Get Christie Love!, *which ran in 1974-75. The three references are all linked.*

First, they are to strong women. One of the lines of Like a Virgin *runs 'Make me strong, yeah you make me bold' (although we do not hear it); the 'sister' in Vicki Lawrence's song is a serial killer; and Christie Love was portrayed as a hard, karate-chopping detective, her well-known punch-line being 'You're under arrest, Sugar', as is recalled by Nice Guy Eddie to the approval of Orange, Pink and White. Second, all of these women are associated with popular music. Third, the anxiety that references to strong women singers might arouse is counteracted in various*

$$\frac{\text{song}}{\text{visuals}} \ \| \ \frac{\text{woman}}{\text{man}} \ \| \ \frac{\text{ear}}{\text{body}}$$

ways. In the case of Madonna, it is the director himself who insists, indeed over-insists that the song is about the pain a woman must feel ('dick dick dick', Tarantino/Mr Brown repeats insistently, to which Mr Blue says, 'How many dicks was that?, and Mr White responds, 'A lot'). In the case of The Night the Lights Went Out in Georgia, *Nice Guy Eddie insists that he had not understood that it was about a woman killer. In the case, finally, of* Get Christie Love!, *no-one can remember Teresa Graves's name, and she is confused with the blaxploitation actress Pam Grier, who was to star in Tarantino's* Jackie Brown.[8] *The film, in other words, tries to undermine the power of the strong women it cannot refrain from evoking, all of whom are associated with song. In this context, severing the ear amounts to a reclaiming of an object associated with the maternal by its connection with song.*

Cutting the ear is therefore cutting off the maternal, abjecting it, turning it into an object of disgust: 'whatever I am, I am not this disgusting object which reminds me of the songs my mother used to sing'. This might appear to be very different from the connotations of the ear in Blue Velvet, *as discussed by Chion, who associates it not with the feminine, but with masculine communication. Chion explains how in* Blue Velvet *there is a strong Œdipal relationship between Frank (Dennis Hopper) and Jeffrey (Kyle MacLachlen), and that one way they communicate is through the ear which Frank has cut off Dorothy (Isabella Rossellini)'s husband:*

[107]

> The ear is the gift bequeathed to Jeffrey by the father. More than the female orifice which leads
> to a closed interior, the ear functions here as a passageway, the symbol of communication
> between two worlds. The ear transmits the gift of passing through the surface, of travelling
> between worlds, then of recovering a normal world (...). Frank thus offers Jeffrey a key to life
> and a gift of imagination. In short, everything in Blue Velvet has a dynamic sense of life, and
> love really is everywhere.

> *(Chion, 1995, p. 97)*

However, I will now go on to show how Chion's view of the ear in Blue Velvet *is not at variance
with the view I am espousing here. Indeed, the ear, I shall attempt to show, is not the 'female
orifice' we might have associated with maternally-connoted song, but a faecalised orifice. It is the
abjected anus, rejected precisely because it functions as the means of communication between
the dogs.*

*Willis discusses the ear-cutting scene and points out how it, and Tarantino's films more generally,
function to embarrass the spectator: 'To be caught laughing when something horrific happens,
gasping at the mismatch between our affective state and the next image, reproduces or recalls
the embarrassment, or even shame, of being caught in a breach of social discipline' (Willis,
2000, p. 281). She extrapolates from this view of oxymoronic scenes being the equivalent of
'getting caught with your pants down', to a more general 'metaphorics of shit', in which spilt
blood signifies the smearing of shit:*

> Part of the reason that bloodletting can be humorous in Tarantino's work is that blood really
> operates likes faeces, so that spilling of blood is very much like smearing. In all its evocation
> of infantile activity, smearing not only provokes laughter, but also implies violence. Though this
> connection between blood and shit might seem at first far-fetched, a look at Tarantino's signa-
> ture effects suggests that it is not. While the celebratory clamour about his emergence as the
> American auteur for the 1990s turns on his wizardry with violence and its eroticised possibil-
> ities, the filmmaker's own appearance as a figure in his films is as closely associated with shit
> as with violence. Tarantino's character in Reservoir Dogs loudly proclaims this in so many
> words. Complaining to his boss about his alias, Mr Brown, he asserts: 'Brown, that's a little too
> close to shit'.

> *(Willis, 2000, p. 281)*

*If we adopt Willis's 'metaphorics of shit', as explored in this passage, we can perhaps see how
the ear can be viewed as an externalised anus, leaking faecal blood. It is the hole made flesh, a*

mode of communication between the two men within the abject, as the 'Hey, hear that?'/'Hey, what's going on?' dialogue suggests (Appendix shot 20).

This view may seem at odds with the notion that the ear represents an abjected maternal object. How can the ear function both as a rejected maternal object and as a masculinised anus? How can an object which we might well have wanted to metaphorise as, precisely, the 'female orifice' by its association with maternalised song, also function as an anal orifice by its association with faecalised smearing? Before answering, we need to remember the highly erotic connotations of the scene. There is Mr Blonde's soft-shoe shuffle which is a kind of seductive show as Mr Blonde acts out the murderous blonde femme fatale; has he not introduced himself to the cop saying 'I think I'm parked in the red zone', with its obvious connotations of transgression, but also of sexual transgression, the 'red district' being the zone of the prostitutes, those who, like him in front of the cop, stand out and in front of, as the etymology of the word, pro-stare, has it? There is his writhing on the cop's lap, which simulates coitus. There is his pointedly sexualised comment after the severing of the ear: 'Was that as good for you as it was for me?', which associates dismemberment with orgasm.

The ear can function bivalently if we place it in the context of Freud's theory of cloacal birth, whereby the boy-child fantasises that he has been born from the mother's anal orifice. Calvin Thomas brings together Freud's account of the fort/da game, and his theory of cloacal birth ('It is a universal conviction amongst children that babies are born from the bowel like a piece of faeces: defecation is a model of the act of birth'; Freud quoted in Thomas, 1996, p. 85) to suggest that the former 'is implicated not only with the boy's fantasy of having been produced through his mother's bowels, and his foreclosure of that fantasy, but also with his own struggles to secure identity through the control of his bowels' (Thomas, 1999, p. 29). As Thomas points out, those struggles are never really successful, and all modes of representation are, to use his word, haunted by scatontological anxiety: 'The image of "unimpaired masculinity", the self-produced, self-representational image of the actively "self-made man", is haunted by the earlier phantasmatic image of having been a passively and cloacally (m)other-made child' (Thomas, 1999: 29). Where have we heard those words, 'self-made man', before ? In the apparently innocuous 'pop bubble-gum' lyrics of Stuck in the Middle With You: 'You started off with nothing,/And you're proud that you're a self-made man'. The combination of apparently innocuous song and violent images is, I am contending, what Thomas calls a 'scatological fantasy', an ontology of shit ('I am because I shit on you').

[109]

But this fecalised space is an all-male space in which women have no (body)part to play. There is a total absence of women, which is not surprising for a heist movie; perhaps more surprising in a film which opens by talking at length about female singers, there are no female voices inside the hangar. The only one we hear in this sequence, again very pointedly, is a woman's laughter outside *the hangar when Mr Blonde goes to fetch the petrol-can and the song fades away (Appendix shot 21). If the scene is pushing us to an enactment of cloacal birth, then it is birth without a mother. The maternal vagina is not just replaced by an anal birth-canal; it has been radically expelled from this all-male space leaving a grotesque, abjected anus. The space threatened by femininity and song has been masculinised, and woman written out of the equation, which now reads:*

But for woman to be written out, the men must abject themselves in the feminine, becoming feminised. Mr Blonde, as we have seen, becomes the masquerading femme fatale, and the cop is feminised, his ear an analised vagina, brandished as the offending source of maternal song by Mr Blonde. In other words, in Tarantino's men-only world, men become women and give birth to each other-establish their identities-through the anus. Fecalisation has a triple function, which we can identify in a perverse syllogism:

$$\frac{\text{song}}{\text{visuals}} \; \| \; \frac{\text{woman}}{\text{man}} \; \| \; \frac{\text{ear}}{\text{body}} \; \| \; \frac{\text{man}}{\text{man}}$$

[110]

*   *It abjects the feminine body (the ear), making it into a thing of disgust.*

*   *By the same token it retains the feminine function of procreation, albeit cloacal creation with another man.*

*   *The disgust associated with the abject object protects the male from the abjected feminine and from the homosexualisation implied in cloacal creation with another man. Disgust is in reality a displacement for desire.*[9]

Put more simply, cutting the cop's ear off is like copulation, and the product is identity, a turning into a 'self-made man', a man who makes himself what he is without the help of the mother, but with the help of another man.

Our final equation should therefore read:

The Tarantinian subject is both woman and man, but he is also neither of them. He is a subject in-between, stuck in the middle, 'self-made', in the gap between woman and man, the anal space in-between the two parentheses in the formula above, (wo) and (man).

$$\frac{\text{song}}{\text{visuals}} \parallel \frac{\text{woman}}{\text{man}} \parallel \frac{\text{ear}}{\text{body}} \parallel \frac{\text{(wo)(man)}}{\text{(wo)(man)}}$$

Where does that leave the viewer-listener, apart from being disrupted and confused ? That is precisely where it does leave us: disrupted and confused in our gender roles, abjected, as a result of the disgust engendered by 'gratuitous' and excessive violence. Paradoxical though it may seem, song feminises the dogs as well as abjecting them, and us in the process. We may well reject that feminisation by walking out, but some at least embrace it, the 'groupie' Doggies, midway between the homosocial of male bonding (if we assume that the Doggies are likely to be men) and the homosexual, as implied by the sexual pleasure of abjection, where these men can (re)imagine themselves getting their kicks.

The scene of the crime is therefore 'the men's room', where men not only get their kicks but also 'kick the shit' out of each other, thus making themselves what they are. It is also a room where men play at being mothers, re-birthing themselves violently as abject turds: 'lend me your ear, and I'll make a man/turd of you'. The end-product is, as Sharon Willis might say, nothing more than shit, trash, residue, a point also made in Bataillean mode by Botting and Wilson:

[111]

> If Reservoir Dogs has any reference it is, perhaps, to the condition of sovereignty and abjec-
> tion, to what, in a restricted economy of use and exchange, is held in reserve, the surplus, the
> profit and the value that serves no useful function, unemployable and unworkable, the dogs,
> the remains, leftovers of another world of desire, the thieving rabble, the detritus and utter
> waste of expenditure.

(Botting & Wilson, 2001, pp. 70-71).

And who then is there, 'stuck in the middle' with the singer of the song? It is the split subject, forever wondering, wandering forever, leaking excessively across boundaries, shuttling to and fro between man and woman, vagina and anus, sung and seen, ear and here; never being anywhere else than 'there', in the empty space of an impossible, fantasised cloacal (re)birth, stuck in the middle, half-way between fort *and* da, *half-way between diarrhoea and constipation, a black-clad reservoir turd, 'a little too close to shit', as Tarantino himself observed.*

The song, which as we have shown, functions bivalently, both supports this in-betweenness and counteracts it. Like the singer of the song, we are in a bowel-like space surrounded by jokers and clowns, afraid of falling, of losing control; afraid then of faecalisation, of being placed in the lawless pre-Œdipal, infantile world of smearing with all the pleasure to be had in shit. Like the singer of the song, we are at the same time 'self-made men', in the Œdipal world, the space of the law, abjecting those bad objects (the ear, the 'dogs') which help us to define who we would like to be, with all the satisfaction to be had in being able to treat those objects with disgust. The song, so apparently innocuous and anodine, is therefore far more complex than would at first seem. Like the process I have just described, it is neither 'Dylanesque' nor 'pop bubble-gum', neither 'male' nor 'female', but somewhere in-between. It is key to negotiating a viewing-hearing position in which disgust and desire reinforce each other and guarantee the disintegrated integrity of our viewing and hearing experience.[10]

Notes

[1] *'A reporter asks Tarantino why there are no women in the film. I choke back a snort; the movie practically wears a placard saying Girls Keep Out. (There are two women, onscreen long enough for one to shoot somebody before she's shot herself, while another is pulled through the driver's window of her own car and left sprawling in the road.) "It would be like women turning up on the submarine in Das Boot", Tarantino answers sweetly, "There's no place for women in this movie"' (Taylor, 2000, p. 21).*

[2] *See Peary, 1998, p. 29; Brunette, 1998, p. 33; Tarantino, 2000, p. 30.*

[3] *See Appendix shot 12. In fact, the song was released in April 1973 in the USA, reaching number six there, and number eight in the UK in May of that year (Barnes & Hearn 1996, p. 142). 'Dylanesque' may refer to Gerry Rafferty's slightly nasal tone, but equally to Dylan's 'Stuck Inside Of Mobile With Memphis Blues Again' from the 1966 Blonde on Blonde album. However, despite some superficial parallels ('And the ladies treat me kindly/And furnish me with tape/But deep inside my heart/I know I can't escape'), Dylan's song is more a drug-induced hallucination of a particular community, whereas the protagonist of 'Stuck in the Middle With You' is ontologically distanced from those around him whom he despises. A second issue with the statement 'Dylanesque pop bubble-gum' is that it is likely to be perceived by those who know Dylan's work as an oxymoron, since his work is the antithesis in both musical and ideological terms of what might be understood as 'pop bubble-gum', a term more likely to be associated with 'inauthenticity' (and 'femininity') than 'authenticity' (and 'masculinity'). The song itself is arguably midway between 'Dylan' and 'pop bubble-gum'; the lyrics, although simple, are complex enough to allow for multilevel readings. At the literal level they suggest the state of drunkenness, and at the figurative level the awareness of being stuck in 'life's party'. Moreover, the music is texturally and timbrally complex; its recognizable lyrical and musical repetitions reinforce both of these levels. The film's attempt to structure a gendered binary (the song as feminine and the visuals as masculine) is problematic, as we shall see. (I am grateful to Robynn Stilwell for these points.)*

4 I am grateful to Robynn Stilwell for helping me tease out the problems inherent in the gendered binary, and for providing the formulations here.

5 The fact that the ear is a disembodied (w)hole is emphasised by one of the most remarkable aspects of the scene's mise-en scène: the ten-second hold on the empty door-frame at the back of the hangar as the ear is severed, and into which Mr Blonde eventually soft-shoe shuffles, ear-first; see Appendix shot 19. We shall see below the significance of the filling of one hole (the door-frame) by another hole (the severed ear), and their associations with a rear position (the door-frame is at the back of the hangar).

6 One way of doing this is to search for intertextual references, suggesting a 'tradition' of severed ears. Thus, a Tarantino encyclopaedia lists Django (Corbucci, 1966); Blue Velvet (Lynch, 1986); The Last Temptation of Christ (Scorsese, 1988); and Carry on Columbus (Thomas, 1992), as well as Van Gogh films such as Lust for Life (Minnelli, 1956); Vincent (Cox, 1987); and Vincent and Theo (Altman, 1990) (to which they could have added the French Van Gogh (Pialat, 1991)). Coincidences are turned into teleological evidence, as we are reminded that Vincent and Theo starred Tim Roth, and The Last Temptation of Christ's ear-cutting happened in the presence of Harvey Keitel as Judas, both of whom have major roles in Reservoir Dogs. We are being told that ear cutting in Reservoir Dogs was inevitable and in the logic of a mythos (see Barnes & Hearn, 1996, pp. 49-50). They do suggest that Blue Velvet is the most important of these films for Reservoir Dogs, but do not give reasons why. We shall return to Blue Velvet below.

[113]

7 I am grateful to Ian Biddle for these formulations.

8 MR PINK: What the fuck was the name of the chick who played Christie Love?
EDDIE: Pam Grier.
MR ORANGE: No, it wasn't Pam Grier, Pam Grier was the other one. Pam Grier did the film. Christie Love was like a Pam Grier TV show, without Pam Grier.
MR PINK: So who was Christie Love?
MR ORANGE: How the fuck should I know?
MR PINK: Great, now I'm totally fuckin' tortured.

9 A point made by _i_ek: 'Disgust occurs when we get too close to the object of desire (...). Pleasure and disgust are (...) related just like the seeming two sides of the continuous Moebius strip; if we proceed far enough on the side of pleasure, all of a sudden we find ourselves in disgust' (_i_ek & Dolar, 2002, pp. 144-45). The note which follows this observation is revealing in the context of the scene we are exploring: 'Bands of homophobic thugs often gang rape their gay victims to humiliate them, thereby committing the very act for which they (pretend to) despise them' (_i_ek & Dolar, 2002, p. 149, n. 20).

10 *I am grateful to Ian Biddle and Robynn Stilwell for their productive comments on a draft of this chapter.*

11 *The filmscript has the following note at this point: 'This entire sequence is timed to the music.' This is followed by brief stage directions which do not reflect the detail of the sequence: 'Mr. Blonde slowly walks toward the cop. He opens a large knife. He grabs a chair, places it in front of the cop and sits in it. Mr. Blonde just stares into the cop's/our face, holding the knife, singing along with the song. Then, like a cobra, he LASHES out. A SLASH across the face. The cop/camera moves around wildly. Mr. Blonde just stares into the cop's/our face, singing along with the seventies hit. Then he reaches out and CUTS OFF the cop's/our ear. The cop/camera moves around wildly. Mr. Blonde holds the ear up to the cop/us to see. Mr. Blonde rises, kicking the chair he was sitting on out of the way.'*

References

Barnes, A. & Hearn, M. *Tarantino A to Zed: The Films of Quentin Tarantino*. London: B.T. Batsford, 1999.

Bernard, J. *Quentin Tarantino: The Man and His Movies*. London: Harper Collins, 1995.

Botting, F. & Wilson, S. *The Tarantinian Ethics*. London: Sage, 2001.

Brunette, P. (1998) 'Interview with Quentin Tarantino', in Peary, G. (Ed.), *Quentin Tarantino: Interviews*. Jackson: University Press of Mississippi, pp. 30-34.

Chion, M. *David Lynch*. London: BFI, 1995.

Ciment, M. & Niogret, H. (1998) 'Interview at Cannes', in Peary, G. (Ed.), *Quentin Tarantino: Interviews*. Jackson: University Press of Mississippi, pp. 9-26.

Kristeva, J. (1982) *Powers of Horror: An Essay on Abjection*, Roudiez, L. S. (trans.), New York: Columbia University Press. Originally published 1980.

McCarthy, T. (2000) 'Reservoir Dogs', in Woods, P. (Ed.), Quentin Tarantino: The Film Geek Files. London: Plexus, pp. 16-17. Originally published in Variety, January, 1992.

Mannoni, O. (1969) 'Je sais bien, mais quand même', in Clefs *pour l'Imaginaire. Paris* : Seuil, pp. 9-33.

Metz, C. (1982) *Psychoanalysis and Cinema: The Imaginary Signifier*. London: Macmillan.

Peary, G. (1998) 'A Talk with Quentin Tarantino', in Peary, G. (Ed.), *Quentin Tarantino: Interviews*. Jackson: University Press of Mississippi, pp. 27-29.

Tarantino, Q. (2000) 'It's cool to be banned', in Woods, P. (Ed.), *Quentin Tarantino: The Film Geek Files*. London: Plexus, pp. 30-31.

Taubin, A. (2000) 'The Mens Room', in Woods, P. (Ed.), *Quentin Tarantino: The Film Geek Files*. London: Plexus, pp. 26-29. Originally published in Sight and Sound, December, 1992.

Taylor, E. (2000) 'Mr Blood Red', in Woods, P. (Ed.), *Quentin Tarantino: The Film Geek Files*. London: Plexus, pp. 19-25. Originally published in *L.A.Weekly*, October, 1992.

Thomas, C. (1996), *Male Matters: Masculinity, Anxiety, and the Male Body on the Line*. Urbana & Chicago: University of Illinois Press.

Thomas, C. (1999) 'Last laughs: Batman, masculinity and the technology of abjection', *Men and Masculinities*.2:1, pp. 26-46.

Willis, S. (2000) '"Style", posture, and idiom: Tarantino's figures of masculinity', in Gledhill, C. and Williams, L. (Eds.), *Reinventing Film Studies*. London: Arnold, pp. 279-95.

Woods, P. (1998), *King Pulp: The Wild World of Quentin Tarantino*. London: Plexus, 1998.

Woods, P. (2000) *Quentin Tarantino: The Film Geek Files*. London: Plexus.

Zizek S. and Dolar, M. (2002), *Opera's Second Death*. New York and London: Routledge.

Appendix

In the following shot description, I am taking the sequence from midway through the first shot as Eddie, White and Pink exit the warehouse leaving Blonde to look after the cop. I am terminating the sequence mid-shot at the end of the song. Each shot is numbered and contains a description of what can be seen, as well as what can be heard. The published film-script's dialogue and stage directions are not accurate.

1. Long shot. Mr Blonde watches Eddie, White and Pink exit the warehouse, jumps off the boxes where he was sitting, and takes off his jacket. *MR BLONDE: Alone at last.*

2. Close-up dolly of Mr Blonde walking towards the cop.

3. POV dolly towards the cop.

4. Close-up dolly of Mr Blonde walking towards the cop.

5. POV dolly towards the cop., who spits blood as Mr Blonde arrives in front of him.

6. Mr Blonde stands over the cop, smoking a cigarette. *MR BLONDE: Guess what. I think I'm parked in the red zone. (He laughs.) Now where were we?*

7. Camera tracks and pans left around from behind Mr Blonde to end up behind the cop's right shoulder as the cop speaks. *COP: I told you I don't know anything about any fucking set up. I've been on the force for only eight months, they don't tell me anything! Nobody tells me shit. You can torture me all you want.*

8. Mr Blonde walks backwards and forwards in front of the cop. *MR BLONDE: Torture you, that's a good, that's a good idea, yeah, I like that one, yeah. (He brushes his trousers.) COP: Even your boss said there wasn't a set up. MR BLONDE: My what? COP: Your boss. (Mr Blonde flicks away his cigarette.) MR BLONDE: Excuse me pal.*

One thing I want to make clear to you. I don't have a boss. Nobody tells me what to do. Understand?

9.   Close-up of cop. He slaps the cop's face. *MR BLONDE: You hear what I say, you son of a bitch? COP: Alright, alright, you don't have a boss, alright.*

10.   Mr Blonde walks backwards and forwards in front of the cop, shaking the cop's sweat and blood off his hand, and then rubbing it on the cop's left shoulder. *MR BLONDE: What the fuckin' shit.* (He picks up some tape from a bench on the side of the room and walks back.) *Look kid, I'm not going to bullshit you, OK? I don't really give a big fuck what you know or don't know.* (He smiles and undoes the tape.) *But I'm gonna torture you anyway, regardless.* (He tears off a strip of tape.) *Not to get information.* (He throws the tape back onto the bench with a bang, and goes behind the cop.) *It's amusing to me to torture a cop. You can say anything you want, because I've heard it all before.* (He puts a piece of tape over the cop's mouth.) *All you can do is pray for a quick death, which...you ain't gonna get.* (He draws his gun on the cop, who struggles. Mr Blonde chuckles. Mr Blonde walks away from the cop.)

11.   Close-up of Mr Blonde's boot on the edge of the bench as he draws out a flick-knife and opens it; shot ends with Mr Blonde's face in close-up disappearing out of shot. *MR. BLONDE: Ever listened to K-Billy's 'super sounds of the seventies'?*

12.   Mr Blonde crouches down. *MR BLONDE: It's my personal favourite.* (He turns on the radio and as the DJ introduces the song he walks in front of the cop pretending to shave himself, ending up by crouching down by Mr Orange.) *DJ K BILLY: 'Joe Egan and Gerry Rafferty were a duo known as Stealer's Wheel when they recorded this Dylanesque pop bubble-gum favourite from April of 1974. They reached up to number 5, as K-Billy's super-sounds of the 70s continues.'* (Mr Blonde lifts Mr Orange's suit, and looks up at the cop smiling as the song starts.)[11]

13.   Close-up of cop's face looking at Mr Blonde.

14.   Mr Blonde stands and shuffles to and fro as he sings along.
        SONG: Well, I don't know why I came here tonight, I got the feeling...

15.   Close-up of cop's face looking at Mr Blonde.
        ...that something ain't right. I'm so scared in case I fall off...

16.   Mr Blonde stands and shuffles to and fro as he sings along.

...my chair,
And I'm wondering how I'll get down the stairs.
Clowns to the left of me, jokers to the right,
Here I am, stuck in the middle with you.
*Yes, I'm...(*Mr Blonde stops in front of the cop and slashes his face.*)*

17.   Close-up of cop's face as it is slashed and he screams with pain; he will carry on
        with muffled screams throughout the song.
        ...stuck in the middle with...

18.   Mr Blonde holds the cop's face as the cop struggles (camera behind cop).
        ...you,
        And I'm...

19.   Mr Blonde holds the cop's face as the cop struggles (camera behind Mr Blonde).
        ...wondering what it is I should do.
        He crouches down in front of the cop. We realize that he is cutting off the cop's
        ear, but Mr Blonde's body hides the action.
        It's so hard to keep this smile from my face,
        The camera pans left onto an opening in the wall behind on which it remains fixed
        for ten seconds while sounds of scuffling accompany the cop's muffled screams.
        Losing control, yeah, I'm all over the place.
        Clowns to the left of me, jokers to the right,
        Here I am, stuck in the middle with you.
        Mr Blonde returns to shot looking at the cop's ear in his left hand.
        Well, you started off with nothing,
        And you're proud that you're a self-made man.
        And your friends they all come crawlin',
        Slap you on the back and say, 'Please, please.'
        On the first 'please' he walks out of shot back to the cop and we hear him off-
        screen. *MR BLONDE: Was that as good for you as it was for me?*

20.   Mr Blonde stands over the cop who is still writhing in pain. *MR BLONDE* (into the
        cop's severed ear): *Hey, what's goin' on?* (To the cop, laughing, as the second
        'please' is heard.) *Hey, hear that?* (Mr Blonde throws away the ear and wipes his
        left hand on the cop's right shoulder. The third verse of the song starts during the
        following dialogue.) *Don't go anywhere. I'll be right back.*
        Trying to make some sense of it all,
        But I can see...

[117]

21.   Fast left pan and forward-moving hand-held camera follows Mr Blonde as he exits
        the warehouse to the car outside.
        ...it makes no sense at all.
        Is it cool to go to sleep on the floor?
        Well, I don't think I can take any more.
        Clowns to the left of me, jokers to the right,
        Here I am, stuck in the middle with you.
        The music fades away as we hear his footsteps and distant female laughter. He
        takes a canister of petrol out of the boot of the car and the camera follows him
        back into the warehouse. The music fades back in at 'please, please'.
        (Well, you started out with nothing,
        And you're proud that you're a self-made man.
        And your friends they all come crawlin',
        Slap you on the back and say,) 'Please, please.'
        Mr Blonde shuffles around the room towards the cop.
        Yeah, I don't know why I came here tonight,

        I got the feeling that something ain't right,
        I'm so scared in case I fall off my chair,
        And I'm wondering how I'll get down the stairs,
        Clowns to the left of me...

22.   Mr Blonde throws petrol into the cop's face (hand-held camera).
        ...jokers to the right,
        Here I am, stuck in the middle with you.

23.   Close-up of cop's face as Mr Blonde throws petrol into it a second time (hand-held
        camera).
        Yes I'm stuck...

24.   Mr Blonde circles clockwise around the cop sprinkling petrol on him and finishes by
        throwing it into the cop's face a third time.
        ...in the middle with you,
        Stuck in the middle with you,
        Here I am, stuck in the middle with you.

25.   Close-up of cop's face as Mr Blonde rips off the tape which had become unstuck.
        COP: Don't!

26.   Mr Blonde throws away the tape. *COP: Stop! (*The music stops.*) Stop. MR BLONDE: What? What's the matter? COP: Don't do this.*

Always Blue: Chet Baker's Voice *John Roberts*

Almost Blue [Chet Baker, 1988] / Let's Get Lost [Bruce Webber, 1988]

Always Blue: Chet Baker's Voice

John Roberts

In the early part of his career Chet Baker's singing was regularly attacked by jazz critics and jazz cognoscenti for its would-be feeble and winsome quality. The followers of abrasive East Coast be-bop thought his range narrow and effeminate. His fellow musicians were not much more sympathetic either. When he recorded Chet Baker Sings in 1954 he frustrated his backing band and producer by having to do dozens of takes of each song. He was hesitant and subdued. In Paris at the beginning of a French tour in 1955 at Salle Pleyel he was even given the 'bird'. This affected him badly and he hardly sang on stage for the rest of the tour. As a result he was prone to question his singing during this period. But during the tour an event occurred that had the most profound affect on his life, his music, and even, it might be said, the future development of his vocal abilities and their place within his trumpet repertoire. A friend of his, Richard 'Dick' Twardzik, who was also the pianist on the French tour, died of a heroin overdose. Baker had only known Twardzik briefly yet considered him one of the greatest musicians he had ever played with and moreover someone who he felt a strong and overwhelming emotional attachment towards. By this time Baker was himself doing heroin, and it has been suggested that Baker was actually with Twardzik when he died. Baker denied this repeatedly, but left enough clues in interviews to suggest he was involved in some deception. Anyway, whether Baker was with Twardzik or not, the death traumatized him and certainly contributed to the increase in his own use of heroin. In this regard it was clear that the death produced a powerful emotional response in his music during this time and after. In what turned out to be kind of memorial concert in London a few days after Twardzik's death, Baker gave an all-vocal performance of plaintive love songs at the Stoll Theatre in memory of his friend, which he cut short after fifteen minutes because of obvious grief.[1] Ironically he was forced to sing because of a British musicians' union ban at the time on American instrumentalists; yet the turn to singing again in these fraught circumstances seems to have produced a defining moment in how he used his voice, its qualities of grace and understatement, and in turn how he defined his public persona through choosing to building a career out of the interpretation of the modern love song. From this point onwards the plangent song of failed or doomed love becomes a defining part of his career as trumpet player. Indeed, as a trumpeter and singer Baker becomes first and foremost an interpreter of the cadences and melody of the song. At no point in his career does he follow Miles Davis in exploring the modern repertoire of the trumpet, or experiment in post-bebop jazz forms. Of course, the forlorn and mournful qualities of Baker's trumpet playing and singing were already in place by 1954-1955; and in this sense it is not the loss of his friend that is instrumental in drawing him to the interpretation of the love song. Yet the loss of Twardzik, and the loss of the possibility of making what he considered to be the 'best' music with his friend, seems to have generated a moment of painful irreconcilability, pushing his vocalization on into another register, a place where the *uncertainties about his vocal abilities become obvious strengths. This is immediately evident in his recording of* Everything Happens to Me *in November 1955 when he returns to Paris after the English tour - the first recording on which Baker sings without accompanying himself on trumpet. Slightly maudlin and self-pitying, the singing nevertheless is confident and beautifully modulated. But this shift is perhaps more evident in the collection of songs recorded in 1957, which was eventually released in 1995 after his death, as* Embraceable You. *With its soft, lilting versions of various vocal standards, such as* The Night We Called it a Day *and* Forgetful, *the album sees Baker exploring in a restrained yet fluid fashion the melancholic possibilities of the sentimental ballad and torch song. Considered to be too depressing on completion to be released, it nevertheless gives a clear insight into how Baker's melancholic delivery was beginning to define something bigger than his own preferences for slow, tentative ballads and his precious cultivation of 'cool'. Baker's fan base at this time already consisted of a large number of young women who loved the 'wounded' aura of his voice, trumpet playing, and of course his appearance: handsome, bruised and vulnerable. The increased presence of the love song in his repertoire, then, found an immediate resonance amongst his growing female audience. It is not too hard to imagine, therefore, that in finding a sympathetic audience quite different from the largely male be-bop crowd he felt more confident about the place of the melancholic love song in his repertoire. In this respect in a jazz industry in the 1950s dominated by hard, aggressive definitions of value in jazz, his early female audience created an influential space of development for his 'feminized' vocalization. Gerry Mulligan, his earlier stage partner and, later, rebarbative critic, was, however, less sympathetic at the time. He dismissed Baker's aura as the result merely of his chronic limitations as a singer: the melancholic allure was just the way he sang, no more nor less. This maybe the case, but Mulligan misses an important point about the relationship between technique and the emotional content of music: limited technique does not exclude expressive power, in fact, limited technique can increase and concentrate such power. And this was why Baker's development as a singer was latterly so successful. His would-be limited range opened up an extraordinary space of identification for the listener. This is why he was also one of the few musicians of the period to develop a gay following, albeit clandestinely. His self-mortification and ghostly pacification on record, coupled with William Claxton's glamorous photographs of him in the recording studio, created a palpable world of gay desire and loss. It was if his gay audience intuited what Baker's close friends also intuited: that he was actually singing his songs for Twardzick. Baker was always dismissive of the homoerotic reception of his music - violently so sometimes. But it is clear that the feminized expression of his voice contributed to his popular success in the fifties and early sixties, particularly during the mid-fifties when magazine editors, record producers and film producers were keen to identify Baker with the new 'feminized' anti-hero in Hollywood-cinema (James Dean, Marlon Brando). His presentation as a vocalist at this time owes a great deal to the questioning of conventional, masculinities in the new cinema. In short, Baker's voice was able to resonate way beyond its obvious technical limitations to define*

[123]

a realm of subjectivity that evoked other worlds, other feelings, other desires, than those on offer in the hyper-conformist US of the 1950s.

This is the imaginary world that the fashion photographer Bruce Weber re-evoked when he made his documentary Let's Get Lost *about Baker, in 1986: Baker as a forlorn and bittersweet icon of homoerotic and adolescent desire. But in the intervening years this image had largely been replaced by that of Baker, the haunted junkie. From the late fifties to his death in 1988 Baker's public persona was indivisible from his life as a heavy heroin user. This abuse left him ravaged - and not just from the effects of the drugs themselves. In 1966 he lost his embouchure after being severely beaten, reputedly, for the non-payment or late-payment of one too many drug deals. The physical and emotional scars in the 1970s and 1980s seemed all too evident. Yet although the film is a study in decayed beauty and power, it is not a film, thankfully, about the redemption of Chet Baker. Baker wasn't exactly a forgotten or unproductive figure during the 60s, 70s and 80s, he had recorded a huge number of albums, some poor, but some also as good as the early years. Weber realises that he doesn't need our sympathy as a junkie-musician. Rather, the film is concerned with what Baker had achieved in the 50s and 60s and as such what he meant for so many people during that period - and after.* Let's Get Lost, *is a homage to, and re-enchantment of that older image. In this regard it is also film framed by Weber's own desire - his desire for the public image of Baker that the photographer himself remembered from the sixties and that later influenced his own homoerotic photographs for Calvin Klein and other fashion companies.* Let's Get Lost *is as much about the continuing resonance of William Claxton's images - which are a constitutive part of the film and its retrospective pleasures - as it is about the memory of what Baker's music meant for Weber and those non-conformist, lovelorn audiences of the 1950s and 1960s. Indeed, in our imaginary reconstruction of Baker they are inseparable. As such it is a film that uses the past and present image of Baker to open up the melancholic power of the music.*

Documentary films about popular singers usually present the artist in their stage role or persona. The singer and the dynamics of their performance are invariably framed by the demands of the 'star system', that is, by the fable of the artist's expressive self-containment and creative spontaneity. The performer is rarely seen as faltering or unsure in their performance, or seen talking about the technicalities of their singing. In the conventional documentary the talking heads who are hired to offer a judgement on the performer's abilities, speak inevitably, in the language of bland approbation. Of course some documentaries break this rule and encourage self-criticism and scepticism about the star system, particularly when the artist in question wants to encourage an independent image; but in general very few profiled singers are willing or encouraged to talk on film about the complexities and content of their music, or are shown in rehearsal, or reflecting on the experiences that they bring to their music. These are very much now the rules of for TV music documentaries, which have become so ubiquitous in the MTV era: the projected coherence of the singer's public image comes before all critical and musical scrutiny. Bruce Weber's documentary about Baker doesn't necessarily break with the star-making machinery - Weber is too enthralled, too fascinated by the Baker myths and Baker's self-mythologizing to prise Baker's image completely from its glamorous enshrinement in 50s Americana. Yet, at the same time, the film is not a hagiographic account of the musician's professional career or an attempt to separate the realities of the life from the music. Weber draws on the intense and bitter memories of those who knew and loved him, in particular one of his ex-wives, as a counterpoint to Baker's own halting and sometimes painful reflections. The musician is shown in all his deviousness and vulnerability (although his notorious temper flickers only occasionally into view). But this emotional candidness is not what makes Let's Get Lost *such a compelling music documentary. Rather, what contributes to the film's distinctiveness and quality is the dreaminess it evokes by allowing the evocative informality of Baker's singing style to shape the flow of events and accompanying voices. This is a film which uses the forlornness and sweetness of his voice to structure our emotional response to his life and music; overall Baker the trumpeter and virtuoso musician is a secondary presence here. We see him in the studio singing, including* Blame it On My Youth *and* Imagination, *improvising vocally with friends, and at the end of the film at the 1987 Cannes film Festival, performing a slow, dark version of Elvis Costello's* Almost Blue. *This is the musical high point of the film and that moment in the film where Baker's voice gives poignant shape to the life and music on screen. Indeed, if* Let's Get Lost, *is a film overshadowed by the image of Baker from the 1950s, it is also a film overshadowed by the 'brokenness' of Baker's singing voice. The voice of the singer in the conventional documentary music film is usually subordinate to biographical structure of the narrative or to the authority of the disembodied voice-over. In* Let's Get Lost, *there is no voice-over or conventional narration of the artist's musical history, and therefore Baker's spoken and singing voice are able to dominate the sound-track. In other words his spoken voice and singing voice suture the life and the music into an imaginary world. And this is why his version of* Almost Blue *is such a focal emotional point for the film. Weber shoots Baker in close-up, mouth pressed to the microphone, for the duration of the song.*

[125]

So intense is his performance we are not sure whether he will manage to finish the song, or remain standing. His closed eyes, and the intimacy he forces from the microphone, produce a feeling that this song is being sent out into the world as a final valediction. But this is the secret of Baker's vocalization: its capacity to enfold the listener into a direct experiential space. There are not many male singers who have this capacity. This has to do with the unusually solicitous and introspective character of his voice. Baker's 'feminized' intonation removes from the delivery of the song all those qualities of vocal attack and swagger associated with the sexual predatoriness and physical presence of the male popular singer. In the 1950s this obviously would have meant Frank Sinatra and the Nelson Riddle orchestra, but also the jump-jazz of Louis Jordan and the early rock 'n' roll of Elvis Presley, Little Richard, and Jerry Lee Lewis. Baker's voice seems to emanate from another kind of place, a place in which desire is always faltering or out of reach or endlessly painful. No male singer had sung the standards of lost love quite like this. In this way Baker's solicitousness can be compared to what Kleinian-influenced psychoanalysts call the 'good voice', the voice that is soothing and supportive. In Didier Anzieu's work on child development the 'good voice' is identified, predominantly, with that of the mother's. By providing the child with a continuous stream of comforting and non-threatening aural stimulus, the mother produces a 'sonorous envelope' in which the child's ego is able to develop without threat.[2] Inside the sonorous envelope the child is protected against effects of discordant and disruptive stimuli. As such the 'good voice' of the sonorous envelope is contrasted with the 'bad voice' of vocal assault, anger and chaos. But the threat of the 'bad voice' is not just external. The 'bad voice' is also immanent to the child's desires. So when the child's cries of discomfort or anger are consoled by the 'good voice', the 'good voice' is further identified by the child with the stilling of pain and with pleasure and reassurance. The child realises that the presence of the 'good voice' brings comfort. Baker's 'feminized' voice, I would argue, works its effects in this maternal space of the 'good voice'. It is solicitous in a way that evokes the consoling power of the calming mother. But at the same time this is not a voice which is life-affirming or uplifting in any straightforward fashion, as if Baker was singing jazz lullabies. It is also a voice that emerges from disintegrative forces itself. At the heart of the voice's softness we also hear death. For those who were indifferent or antagonistic to Baker's singing in the 1950s and 1960s this was something of a joke: Baker sounded as if was actually about to expire. But clichés about heroin-chic aside,

the melancholy of living-with-the-death-of-desire is intertwined in the delivery of the songs with the voice of someone who knows death, and more to the point, knows how close he himself is daily to its clutches. Baker's voice may have formed itself initially out of the singer's limited range of possibilities, but by the mid-1950s when Baker begins taking heroin, the ego-withdrawing effects of heroin addiction also begin to bring these limitations into emotional focus. That is, the lulling sensuousness of heroin addiction finds an expressive correlate in the plaintive voice. It would make obvious sense to enforce this connection and say that the sonorous envelope of Baker's voice is really the depressed voice of the addict, but this is too easy. Baker was an addict and his voice emanates from that world, but the voice is also captivatingly adolescent in its inflections. And this is what also contributes to the sonorous envelope's solicitous, soothing qualities. The 'feminization' of Baker's voice is almost child-like: Baker sings of love, and of lost love, but his passions are strangely asexual. As Baker got older these qualities darkened and roughened; and it is these we hear so disconcertingly in his performance of 'Almost Blue' in Let's Get Lost. Costello wrote the song especially for Baker, and it represents a kind of pastiche of the songs-for-lovers that made Baker's name in the 1950s. But, in Baker's hands it loses that imitative qualit, and becomes something utterly singular. In the film Baker slows the song down to a spoken, resonant growl. As with many other treatments of songs throughout his career, the spoken song for Baker allows him to deflate the prettiness of the song's sentiments. Costello's song isn't exactly sentimental, but in Baker's hands the lyric about the face of an old lover, whom the singer recognises in the face of another woman, becomes a deathly memorialization of their *love affair. 'All the things that you promised with your eyes I see in hers too'. This is the voice of someone who is aging and fatigued, whose passions are spent and who is recalled to the past through a glimpse of a stranger's face. That Weber places this at the end of* Let's Get Lost *is clearly intended to carry another kind of memorial content: the loss of a younger, vital Baker to the decrepitude of addiction. It as if Baker was singing the final lament to the destruction of his own powers. But, if there is pathos here, there is also self-will and strength. Reputedly Baker had great powers of recovery, which allowed him to overcome the worst ravages of his addiction and we see this in the Cannes hotel performance. Despite Baker's obvious physical frailty the song is performed with an extraordinary forcefulness.*

'Almost Blue' grounds the emotional truth of the film, just as the form of the song carries the biographical content of the narrative. In this Let's Get Lost *is as much about the space of Baker's voice, as it is about the details and travails of the musician's life. Indeed, Baker's musical history seems to be of subsidiary interest to Weber. What structures the film, rather, is that sensuous place where voice and face meet: the evocativeness of song.* Let's Get Lost, *essentially, is about the intoxication of a voice and the beauty of a face and how both, entwined, mark the most intimate place of our pleasures.*

Notes

1   *See James Gavin, Deep in a Dream: The Long Night of Chet Baker, Alfred A Knopf, 2002.*

2   *Didier Anzieu, The Skin Ego, translated by Chris Turner, Yale University Press, 1989.*

From Bond To Blank *Jeff Smith*

Live And Let Die [Wings, 1973] / Grosse Pointe Blank [George Armitage, 1997]

From Bond to Blank

Jeff Smith

When I was first asked to contribute an essay to this volume, I didn't have to give much thought to the film and song that I would discuss. Without hesitation, I responded that I wanted to examine the use of Paul McCartney's Live and Let Die *in* Grosse Pointe Blank *(1996), a quirky comedy about a hit man facing a mid-life crisis when he attends his ten-year high school reunion. Although McCartney's song was originally written for the James Bond classic of the same title, it appears in* Blank *in a very brief scene where the titular hero, Martin Blank, returns to the spot of his childhood home only to learn that it has been turned into a convenience store.[1] By selecting this particular moment of* Blank, *I do not mean to suggest that this is a particularly notable or even memorable use of music in the film.[2] Indeed, while most people I've talked to can vaguely recall the scene itself, almost no one remembers the specific piece of music that accompanies it, namely Guns N' Roses' cover version of the tune from* Use Your Illusion 1. *In this respect, the use of* Live and Let Die *might seem striking in the very ordinariness of its usage. Unlike far more memorable pop moments in films such as Quentin Tarantino's use of* Stuck in the Middle With You *in* Reservoir Dogs *(1994) or Iggy Pop's* Lust for Life *in* Trainspotting *(1996), director George Armitage's spotting of* Live and Let Die *seems much more conventional. The song appears in a relatively brief snippet that excerpts parts of its verse, chorus, and instrumental bridge, and appears to fade out almost as quickly as it surfaces. Unlike the Stealers Wheel tune,* Live and Let Die *is not used for a particularly significant moment in the narrative. Moreover, unlike the Iggy Pop recording,* Live and Let Die *is not given priority as the first piece of music heard in the film. As part of the ongoing flow of the narrative, 'Live and Let Die' is closer to incidental music than* Lust for Life, *whose function is more like the main title cues of classical Hollywood cinema.*

While all of this is true of Live and Let Die *in this sequence, the apparent ordinariness of its placement belies a much more complex textual function. Unlike many pop songs in Hollywood films, which are used to make a simple point about character or setting,* Live and Let Die *functions here at several different levels simultaneously. In its immediate narrative context, the song conveys Blank's rising anger at learning that his family abode has disappeared. At a much broader level, however, the song also reinforces the film's satiric treatment of commodity culture and competition within corporate capitalism. And at still another level, the song intertextually links* Blank *with the James Bond series, a group of films which provide an implicit contrast between John Cusack's verbose, self-abnegating protagonist and the suave, but deadly English hero.[3] Because of its multi-levelled functions, the use of* Live and Let Die *in* Blank *is almost everything that pop music should be in a Hollywood film: clever, ironic, and rich in its textual and intertextual implications.*

Before proceeding to my analysis, let me briefly describe the first few shots of the aforementioned sequence. The music actually sneaks onto the soundtrack over the last shot of the previous sequence, which shows Blank briefly stopping at his high school to speak with an old teacher. During a medium shot of Blank turning away from the camera and exiting screen left, Axl Rose croaks out the start of the song's first verse. The opening phrase, with its evocation of youthful optimism, thus, serves as a sound bridge to the next sequence, which shows Blank returning home. Live and Let Die *continues over the next image, a tracking shot that follows Blank's car as it pulls up to a stop. Blank then gets out of the car and glances offscreen to the right. This is followed by a reverse field cut to an extreme long shot of an Ultimart in the place where Blank's childhood residence was. In the third shot of the sequence, Blank approaches the camera continuing to look suspiciously toward the space offscreen. The song's title phrase, 'Live and let die', appears in the sequence's fourth shot, which shows Blank entering from off left and looking at the Ultimart in the deep background of the image. In the fifth shot, Blank does something of a double take as he glances back at his car and then turns toward the camera, glowering at the convenience store that sits in the space offscreen. The instrumental chorus of the tune begins during the sixth shot of the sequence, which is a long shot of Blank as he walks toward the Ultimart and enters the store. The Guns N' Roses recording ends abruptly on a match on action of Blank entering the interior of the store. It is replaced, however, by Adam Fields' easy listening version of the song, which picks up exactly where the heavy rock recording left off. Framed from a slightly high angle that approximates the position of a store security camera, Blank pauses briefly in the doorway of the store. This is followed by a cut to a medium shot of Blank pacing inside the store, and then approaching the store clerk behind the checkout. As the camera pans right to reframe Blank, he testily asks the clerk what he is doing in the store. Responding to Blank's somewhat inarticulate query, the clerk replies that he is doing a double shift. The Fields recording continues throughout the remainder of the sequence, which features several shots of Blank trying to reach his uncooperative analyst and the surveillance of two ineffectual National Security Agents.*

At the outset, it is worth noting that the Guns N' Roses recording in this scene fulfills one of the most basic functions of film music, namely signifying a character's emotions and point of view. The overall arc of the music mirrors the growing anger and confusion experienced by Blank during this scene. As instruments are added to the simple piano accompaniment that begins the song, the music swells to suggest this increase in emotional intensity. The instrumental break further reinforces Blank's decision to take action through the change to a faster tempo and the arrangement's emphasis on Slash's heavily distorted guitar melodies. In this sense, the film provides a means of reorienting the basic sounds of heavy metal by situating them within a specific narrative context. Broadly speaking, the wailing guitars, thudding backbeats, and thick instrumental textures of heavy metal, which semiotically connote a mixture of rage, lust, desire, *and hope, are directed toward a more particular narrative purpose here, the communication of Martin Blank's emotional turmoil.[4]*

While the music's signification of emotion is quite conventional, its apparent shift from score to source music is not. At least initially, the sequence holds out the possibility that Live and Let Die *is diegetically motivated as music emanating from Blank's car radio. After all, the audience has been primed to expect this from earlier sequences of Blank in his car. For example, an aerial shot of Blank arriving in* Grosse Pointe *is accompanied by the Violent Femmes'* Blister in the Sun. *As is the case with* Live and Let Die, *the Femmes' tune is used as a sound bridge that begins during the previous sequence, but is subsequently revealed to be source music when Blank pops the tape out of his car stereo. Any expectation that the Guns N' Roses recording would be handled in a similar fashion is dispelled when Blank exits the car and starts walking toward the store. The music's status as underscore is further secured by the music's swell during Axl Rose's intonation of the song's title, a device that fills the space of the soundtrack and eliminates any competing ambient sounds.*

As Blank enters the Ultimart, however, the music abruptly shifts registers from non-diegetic to diegetic. The easy listening version of the tune cleverly picks up the last musical phrase heard in the Guns N' Roses recording, a technique borrowed from the opening of Robert Altman's The Long Goodbye *(1973). In that film, Altman moves back and forth between three different recordings of the title song, all of them diegetically motivated. Armitage's deployment of this device, however, adds a filigree not present in the Altman film. By moving from non-diegetic to diegetic, from Guns N' Roses to Muzak, Armitage uses the music in a manner that replicates the immediate experience of his nettled hero. The shift from the bombastic style of Guns N' Roses to the homogenized, sweet instrumental sounds of Adam Fields parallels the hero's experience in which the site of his nostalgia has been converted to a shrine for commodity culture. In the same way that the roughness and rebelliousness of Axl Rose has been defanged and resituated within an aural environment of consumerism, Blank's childhood has been physically erased to make way for beer, soda, cigarettes, and microwave burritos. As Blank puts it during a brief call to Dr. Oatman, his psychiatrist: 'You can never go home again, Oatman, but I guess you can shop there'.*

The song's title, Live and Let Die, *actually amplifies this dimension of consumer capitalism through its apparent reference to the world of hired killers depicted in the film. Beyond the obvious parallel between killing and dying, the title serves as an apt reference to the cutthroat environment that these hit men inhabit. Indeed, the place of hired killers within the global economy is a central conceit of the film, one explored in the film's central subplot involving Grocer's efforts to form a hit man collective.*

The need for such an organization is established within the film's opening sequence during which

Blank assassinates a rival hit man disguised as a bicycle messenger. Although Blank's action was ostensibly taken to protect an unnamed man and his bodyguard from the messenger, it proves to be fruitless when Grocer (Dan Aykroyd) guns down the two men immediately after Blank has completed his assignment. In a brief meeting afterward, Grocer points out the obvious wastefulness involved in having three different assassins involved in a single assignment. Noting that the fall of the Berlin Wall and the breakup of the Soviet Union has flooded the market with suppliers, Grocer suggests that Blank join him in creating a union or trade association of hit men in order to reduce competition for assignments and thereby increase the asking price for each job. The analogy between murder and capitalism is elaborated further when Marcella mockingly suggests that Blank attend his high school reunion in order to network and establish new accounts. And during the film's final gun battle, when Blank and Grocer team up to kill a team of National Security Agents, the latter coyly remarks on the pairs uneasy alliance by quoting the most famous phrase from The Communist Manifesto: *'Workers of the world unite'.*

This broader theme of competition versus cooperation, thus, impacts our understanding of Live and Let Die *within its narrative context. In the Bond film, the title song refers to the brutality and ruthlessness of both Bond and Dr. Kananga (Yaphet Kotto); in* Grosse Pointe Blank, *the narrative linkage of crime and capitalism gives the title an additional layer of meaning by implicitly referring to the Social Darwinist aspects of a pure market economy. Here again, the music's shift from non-diegetic song to diegetically motivated Muzak reinforces this larger dimension of the film. Within the shift, the rockist authenticity of Guns N' Roses is transformed into a pure commodity, a lite version of the song used to encourage the impulse purchases of soft drinks, magazines, and candy bars. The unseen patrons of the Ultimart are, thus, implicated in this Social Darwinist ethic as the target market that hears the entreaties of in store Muzak and falls prey to the soft-sell approach of corporate marketing strategies. The aforementioned stylistic shift from heavy metal to easy listening serves as a neat reminder that contemporary consumer culture depends on marketing strategies that frequently seek the lowest common denominator in an effort to create unthreatening and impersonal shopping environments.*

[133]

Besides refining the meaning of the song's title phrase, its inclusion in Grosse Pointe Blank *also hints at certain parallels between Blank and Bond, between the modern hit man comedy and the classic Cold War espionage series. Indeed, the telephone byplay between Blank and Marcella is strongly reminiscent of the flirtatious dialogues between Bond and Moneypenny throughout the 007 series. Likewise, in another scene early in the film, Blank attempts to kill a target by slowly dripping poison down a thread from above such that it falls into the open mouth of his unsuspecting and sleeping victim. The* mise en scène *and editing of this sequence will undoubtedly seem familiar to fans of* Dr. No, *in which an assassin sends a poisonous spider down a rope so that it will sting and kill a sleeping James Bond. Finally, the violent duel to the death between Blank and a laconic, vaguely foreign-looking thug is evocative of similar confrontations from the Bond series. Think, for example, of the memorable fight scenes between 007 and such villains as Red Grant in* From Russia With Love *(1963), Oddjob in* Goldfinger *(1964), Jaws in* The Spy Who Loved Me *(1977), and Gobinda in* Octopussy *(1981).*

These parallels, however, are used to establish a more important contrast between Bond and Blank. Much of the humour of Grosse Pointe Blank *comes from its domestication of its ruthless and lethal hero. Blank, like Bond, may have 'state of the art' weaponry, wear finely tailored suits, and drive expensive cars, but unlike Bond, he must handle the day to day operations of his enterprise and, even more surprisingly, he comes 'from somewhere' to use Marcella's phrase. Thus,* Grosse Pointe Blank *wrings humour from two different strategies through which it recontextualizes the familiar Bond persona. On the one hand, the film gets chuckles out of several seemingly ordinary, even jejune, details of what it takes to run a murder-for-hire operation as a small business. This motif is established in the film's first shot, which shows Blank using eyewash just before an important hit. Although the juxtaposition initially seems jarring and inappropriate, it springs from a certain quotidian logic that makes intuitive sense. When lining up a target in a rifle scope, one doesn't want to be bothered by redness, blurriness, or tearing in one's eyes. Blank's use of eyewash, thus, becomes a mark of his consummate preparation and professionalism as we see him take steps to ensure that there will be no physical impairment of his ability to complete the task. Humour also arises from several more of these quotidian details as we hear Blank order necessary work supplies, such as ammunition, and are privy to his arrangements with Marcella to pick up his dry cleaning and feed his cat. (Surely, one never thinks of James Bond having to pick up dry cleaning.)*

[134]

On the other hand, Blank *also earns chortles from its classic 'fish out of water' premise in which a highly skilled, well-trained professional killer returns to the place of his origins, an upper middle-class suburb in Detroit. As Marcella puts it, 'I find it amusing that you came from somewhere,' and by returning Blank to his hometown, the film highlights the cultural clash between Blank and his former friends and colleagues. Indeed, Blank's life is so at odds with the social norms and life experience of his suburban past that he is unable to answer even simple questions about his profession. As he prepares to go with Debbie to his high school reunion, Blank practices his party patter, and tries out several alternative career paths in an effort to craft a plausible cover story for himself. Through an almost Freudian chain of associations, Blank initially describes himself as a pet psychiatrist, but goes on to say that he sells couch insurance, that he test markets positive thinking, and that he leads a weekend men's group specializing in ritual killings. By the end of his imagined discourse, Blank is left muttering the brutal truth about himself: 'I'm not married, I don't have any kids, and I'd blow your head off if someone paid me enough.' More often than not, however, Blank simply tells people the truth about his profession knowing that the truth is so unbelievable that those asking will assume he is either joking or mocking them. For example, when Blank says he is a professional killer to Debbie's father, the latter presumes Blank is ribbing him and replies dryly that murder is a 'growth industry.'*

By referencing Bond through Live and Let Die, *Blank implicitly positions itself as a kind of domesticated version of the 007 persona. Although the film clearly operates within its own narrative universe, it also engages in a kind of imaginative speculation that uses Blank as a cypher to explore a series of 'What if...' questions about Bond's cinematic image. What if Bond came from a perfectly ordinary, suburban, middle-class background? What if Bond had a high school girlfriend for whom he still had feelings? How would Bond interact with his old acquaintances, who now lead perfectly ordinary lives as parents, teachers, real estate agents, car salesmen, and home security guards? What if, instead of being a government spy with a license to kill, Bond had been a husband and father? The latter point is given special force in the film during a scene in which Blank is given a classmate's child. As Blank awkwardly holds the baby, director George Armitage underlines their unspoken interaction through a series of brief close-ups that show Blank looking at the child's wide eyes and innocent face. Like Bond, Blank has money, fine clothes, expensive cars, and neat gadgetry, but also like Bond, he has never experienced the simple joys of marriage and fatherhood.*

Coming just after Blank's conversation with an old teacher, the opening verse of Live and Let Die *neatly captures the sense of personal crisis brought on by Blank's high school reunion:*

[135]

> When you were young and your heart was an open book,
> You used to say 'live and let live'
> (You know you did, you know you did, you know you did)
> But if this ever-changing world in which we're living
> Makes you give in and cry,
> Say 'Live and Let Die'.

Like the narratee of Live and Let Die, *Blank's youthful hopes and optimism have given way to a sense of embitterment and lost opportunity. In returning to his hometown, Blank begins to question his values, particularly his materialism and solipsism. Here again, whereas in the Bond film, the song seems to be a simple reference to its hero's ruthlessness, it takes on new meanings within* Grosse Pointe Blank *through its implicit reference to Blank's sense of loss and nostalgia as he searches for an irrecoverable past signified in the film by his absent childhood home.*

In sum, although it is heard in the film for barely more than a couple of minutes, Live and Let Die *enriches the meanings of* Grosse Pointe Blank *at several levels through its textual and intertextual operations. At one level, the cue plays with notions of sound space by juxtaposing an apparently non-diegetic recording of the song by Guns N' Roses with a diegetically motivated* 'easy listening' version of the song by Adam Fields. Besides manipulating the spectator's perception of sound space, though, the shift from non-diegetic to diegetic, from rock to Muzak, also encapsulates the import of this narrative moment by providing an aural parallel to the way in which Blank's childhood home has been converted to a capitalist shrine to consumer convenience. Finally, through its intertextual reference to the James Bond film of the same name, Live and Let Die also establishes a series of comparisons and contrasts between Bond as the quintessential British agent and Blank as his neurotic American counterpart. In an almost perfect example of intertextual symbiosis, Grosse Pointe Blank gives new meaning to the famous Paul McCartney song while the song itself extends and elaborates Blank's central narrative conceit. If only all pop songs in film carried this much emotional weight and abundance of meaning.

Notes

1   *For more on McCartney's work for the James Bond series, see my chapter on the music of Bond in The Sounds of Commerce: Marketing Popular Film Music. New York: Columbia University Press, 1998, pp. 100-130.*

2   *The body of literature on popular music in films has grown exponentially in the past five years. Besides this volume and my The Sounds of Commerce, there are several recent notable works on this topic, including John Mundy, Popular Music on Screen: From Hollywood Musical to Music Video. Manchester: Manchester University Press, 1999; Russell Lack, Twenty-Four Frames Under: A Buried History of Film Music. London: Quartet Books, 1997, pp. 207-231; Anahid Kassabian, Hearing Film: Tracking Identifications in Contemporary Hollywood Film Music. New York: Routledge, 2001; Pamela Robertson Wojcik and Arthur Knight, (Eds.), Soundtrack Available: Essays on Film and Popular Music. Durham: Duke University Press, 2001; K. J. Donnelly, Pop Music in British Film: A Chronicle. London: British Film Institute, 2002; Wendy Everett (2000) 'Songlines: Alternative Journeys in Contemporary European Cinema' in Music and Cinema. edited by James Buhler, Caryl Flinn, and David Neumayer, Hanover: Wesleyan University Press, pp. 99-117.*

3   *For more on James Bond, see Kingsley Amis. The James Bond Dossier. New York: New American Library, 1965; Raymond Benson. The James Bond Bedside Companion. New York: Dodd, Mead, & Co., 1984; Lee Pfeiffer and Philip Lisa. The Incredible World of 007. New York: Citadel Press, 1992, Steven Jay Rubin. The James Bond Films. New York: Arlington House, 1981; Tony Bennett and Janet Woollacott. Bond and Beyond: The Political Career of a Popular Hero. New York: Methuen, Inc., 1987; and James Chapman. License to Thrill: The James Bond Films. New York: Columbia University Press, 1999.*

4   *The best study of the cultural meanings of heavy metal remains Robert Walser's Running With the Devil: Power, Gender, and Madness in Heavy Metal Music. Hanover, New Hampshire: University Press of New England, 1993.*

References

Amis, Kingsley. (1965), *The James Bond Dossier.* New York: New American Library.

Bennett, Tony and Janet Woollacott. (1987), *Bond and Beyond: The Political Career of a Popular Hero.* New York: Methuen, Inc.

Benson, Raymond. (1984), *The James Bond Bedside Companion.* New York: Dodd, Mead, & Co.

Chapman, James. (1999), *License to Thrill: The James Bond Films.* New York: Columbia University Press.

Donnelly, K. J. (2002), *Pop Music in British Film: A Chronicle.* London: British Film Institute.

Everett, Wendy (2000) 'Songlines: Alternative Journeys in Contemporary European Cinema,' in *Music and Cinema*, edited by James Buhler, Caryl Flinn, and David Neumayer. Hanover, New Hampshire: Wesleyan University Press, pp. 99-117.

Kassabian, Anahid. (2001), *Hearing Film: Tracking Identifications in Contemporary Hollywood* Film Music. New York: Routledge.

Lack, Russell. (1997), *Twenty Four Frames Under: A Buried History of Film Music.* London: Quartet Books,. pp. 207-231.

Mundy, John. (1999), *Popular Music on Screen: From Hollywood Musical to Music Video.* Manchester: Manchester University Press.

Pfeiffer, Lee and Philip Lisa. (1992) *The Incredible World of 007.* New York: Citadel Press.

Rubin, Steven Jay. (1981) *The James Bond Films.* New York: Arlington House.

Smith, Jeff. (1998), *The Sounds of Commerce: Marketing Popular* Film Music. New York: Columbia University Press,.

Walser, Robert.(1993) *Running With the Devil: Power, Gender, and Madness in Heavy Metal Music.* Hanover, New Hampshire: University Press of New England.

Wojcik, Pamela Robertson and Arthur Knight, (2001) (Eds.) *Soundtrack Available: Essays on Film and Popular Music.* Durham: Duke University Press.

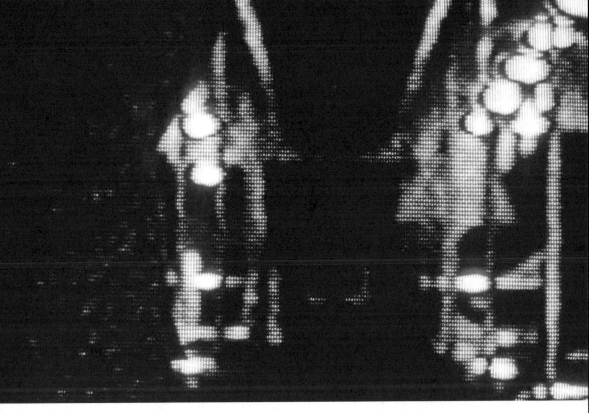

Clean Reading: The Problematics Of 'In The Air Tonight' In Risky Business *Robynn J. Stilwell*

In the Air Tonight [Phil Collins, 1981] / Risky Business [Paul Brickman, 1983]

Clean Reading: The Problematics of 'In the Air Tonight' in Risky Business

Robynn J. Stilwell

1983 was a pivotal year in pop culture. Pop music was recovering from a major sales slump largely on the back of Michael Jackson's massive Thriller. *One key reason for* Thriller's *success was its cross-promotion on MTV, a small cable channel just breaking through to the mainstream. And two films,* Flashdance *and* Risky Business, *appeared which began to put together the modern configuration of cross-media marketing. Both were aimed at young audiences, drawing on the visual style of MTV (which had been, in turn, drawn from television commercials) and cross-promoting the film through the sales of a soundtrack album full of pop songs, then promoting both film and album by the rotation of videos drawn from the movie on MTV, bringing everything in a neat, closed circle. That much is fairly standard knowledge.[1]*

Narratively, Flashdance *is as old as Cinderella and generically little different from a 1930s musical about a girl who goes out there a nobody but comes back a star; the soundtrack album's strategy, however, is forward-looking. It is a collection of pop songs in the vein of films like* Easy Rider *(Dennis Hopper, 1969),* American Graffiti *(George Lucas, 1973), and especially* Saturday Night Fever *(John Badham, 1977), but* Flashdance's *particular success at using MTV through videos comprised of clips from the movie for Irene Cara's title song and Michael Sembello's* Maniac *was revolutionary.*

Narratively and generically, Risky Business *stands at the beginning of the 1980s cycle of teen films more commonly associated with John Hughes films, like* Sixteen Candles *(1984);* The Breakfast Club *(1985);* Pretty in Pink *(1986); and* Ferris Bueller's Day Off *(1986) - a film that is, in some key respects, a more lighthearted version of* Risky Business. *Its soundtrack is poised between eras: it is neither the all-instrumental underscore album that most films spawned in the wake of* Star Wars *(George Lucas, 1977) and* Midnight Express *(Alan Parker, 1978), nor solely a collection of pop songs like* Flashdance. *It is evenly split between instrumental underscore cues by the German electronica band Tangerine Dream, who scored a number of films in the 1980s, and songs by popular artists. In fact, the artists involved in* Risky Business *are all much more prominent than those in* Flashdance, *and ironically, the success of these films would soon make such a soundtrack unfeasible for such a medium-budget film. Certainly today it would be prohibitively expensive to put songs by The Police (who are heard - just barely - in the film, but not on the album), Prince, and Phil Collins into a single film. These are three of the major artists of the 1980s, but they were (with the exception of The Police, who are about to break up) only on the verge of breaking through into the mainstream in 1983.* Risky Business *was marketed through MTV by a video clip - an almost unaltered version of Tom Cruise's famous dance in his* underpants to Bob Seger and the Silver Bullet Band's Old-Time Rock and Roll[2] - but like most of the songs on the soundtrack, this song was already several years old. This was where Risky Business diverged sharply from Flashdance[3] - the use of older, more familiar songs at a time when selling soundtrack albums is not yet a major marketing expectation suggests that the songs are there at least in part for their intrinsic merits.

Phil Collins's minor 1981 hit In the Air Tonight would certainly seem to be such a choice. It is easy to dismiss the use of pop songs as mere marketing tools - it is a common response, and it isn't always wrong. It is also easy to reduce a pop song to its lyrics, or at most its surface style, and sometimes that is all there is to its use in a film. But In the Air Tonight was and remains an unusual pop song, with a strikingly unconventional structure, a haunting and angry sound, and lyrics that border on the psychotic. It is strategically placed at the dramatic peak of the narrative, during the most important love scene in the film, and the song's musical and lyrical strangeness is dissonant with the expectations of the scene. Yet that very dissonance connects on a deeper level with the psychological unease and a trope of surveillance that runs through the film, darkening the tone of what is, on the surface, an adolescent comedy of errors.

The use of In the Air Tonight in Risky Business was also just the first of this song's many appearances at key moments in the popular culture of the 1980s. As the song recurs in different guises, it accrues significance (in both the normative and symbolic meanings of the word).[4] At the same time, the song seems to resist anchorage in any unambiguous meaning. As a result, the song's meaning was already highly unstable within the confines of the film even in 1983, and it becomes almost impossible for audiences coming back to the film today to get a 'clean reading' of this scene, contaminated - or infused - as it is with connections as diverse as Miami Vice and Michelob beer, humanitarianism and war.

[141]

Making Love on a Real Train

Risky Business is notably less frothy than most of the teen comedies with which it is usually grouped. It is the tale of chronic underachiever Joel Goodson (Tom Cruise) who is nearing high school graduation with mediocre grades, a lackluster extra-curricular record, and upper middle-class parents with Ivy League expectations. When his parents leave him alone for the weekend, Joel takes his father's Porsche for a spin which ends up in Lake Michigan, and he gets embroiled in a power struggle between an ambitious young prostitute, Lana (Rebecca de Mornay) and her pimp Guido (Joe Pantoliano). Unlike the ultra-confident Ferris Bueller - who likewise undertakes a picaresque odyssey in a borrowed, expensive sports car and must unravel a series of mishaps, eventually emerging unscathed - Joel stumbles blindly through stupid mistake after stupid mistake (led on mostly by hormones and the egging on by his friend Miles (Curtis Armstrong)), and manages to survive and prosper in large part due to blind luck.

In the Air Tonight *occurs at the point at which all the various threads begin to untangle. Joel and his fellow 'Future Enterprisers' join forces with Lana and her fellow prostitutes to turn the Goodson home into a bordello for the night, servicing all Joel's horny high school colleagues. With the money earned, Joel can pay for the repairs to the Porsche and Lana can break free of Guido (although one major plot obstacle remains as Guido pinches the Goodsons' belongings in revenge). Even Joel's college future is assured when the previously skeptical Princeton admissions officer is impressed by Joel's entrepreneurial prowess - he 'made a few friends' with Lana's colleagues before leaving the house. By this point, Lana has agreed to become Joel's girlfriend, and she wants to 'make love on a real train'.*

It is not just in the narrative that all the threads come together. Symbolically, too, the film has been leading to this point. The movie opens with nocturnal shots of el trains and an eerie, minor-mode synth cue from 'Tangerine Dream'. This might appear merely to be 'establishing' Chicago as the location; but Joel's toy trains also feature in the film, blending the Freudian phallic symbol of the train with the toys emblematic of Joel's immaturity. The psychosexual import of the trains is both playful - it is one of the oldest cinematic tropes for sexuality in the book - and loaded with dark dread: it may be humorous in its obvious symbolism, but Joel is, like most adolescents, as afraid of sex as he is obsessed with it. Both the obviousness of and the fear in the symbolism are further symbolic of his inexperience.

The 'Tangerine Dream' underscore, with its floating, sustained synthesizer timbre and repetitive, yet asymmetrical rhythm vaguely evoking the train, has a hazy, dream-like quality that one can find in a number of fantasy films of the era (notably Giorgio Moroder's score for Paul Schrader's remake of Cat People *(1982) and 'Tangerine Dream's' own scores for* The Keep *(Michael Mann, 1983),* Legend *(Ridley Scott, 1985), and* Near Dark *(Kathryn Bigelow, 1987); even John Carpenter's own score for his 1978 slasher classic* Halloween *and any number of other low-budget horror and fantasy films[5]). The literally unnatural tone of the synthesizer and its ability to sustain and blend tones far beyond the capabilities of traditional instruments seem to create a powerful correspondence between fantasy, unease, and synth scores.*

This musical 'fantasy' trope leads unexpectedly but logically into our introduction to Joel. The opening shots of the el train elide into Joel's narration of a succession of classic psychological fantasy situations: he is lured down a long hall to a beautiful naked girl in the shower, but when he reaches her, he finds himself instead in a classroom about to take his college boards with no preparation - the vaguely ominous 'Tangerine Dream' score continues throughout, the aural equivalent of the steamy haze that only half-logically fills the scene. Sex and terror are even more humorously and potently combined in the first prostitute who shows up at Joel's house - Jackie is a tall, black transvestite with an attitude who has Joel shaking in his sneakers, but she is also his fairy godmother, giving him blonde, blue-eyed Lana's name and number because she knows 'what all you white boys who live on the Lake want.'

The score is one pervasive source of unease in the film; the camera work is another. There are an unusual number of point-of-view shots in the film, starting with Joel's trip down the long hall in his opening fantasy. This disembodied movement through the 'steam' is subtly unsettling; even more disconcerting are the sequences in which the camera takes Joel's place while his parents talk to him. This kind of direct address is uncommon in narrative films, unless in the guise of a 'mockumentary' as in This is Spinal Tap *(Rob Reiner, 1984) or the interview segments of* Strictly Ballroom *(Baz Luhrmann, 1992) where the point of view is explicitly that of a camera. Here, we are without the more comfortable remove of watching the boy squirm under his parents' calm, well-meaning instructions; we are put into his shoes and, cued by his responses from 'behind the camera', supply the squirming ourselves.*

This apparently (deceptively) unmediated gaze is also turned back onto Joel. Not unusually for an adolescent, he has paranoid fantasies of surveillance, from the teacher's disapproving gaze in his college board nightmare to the police and his parents outside the window demanding that he 'get off the babysitter' to Jackie's look piercing his safe home through the peephole. Even his parents' phone calls to check up on him become surveillance, accentuated by their near-direct address into the camera when speaking to him - the audio apparatus of the phone is interposed cinematically by the visual apparatus of the camera, relaying their gaze to the camera to Joel on the other end of the line. None of these shot constructions in and of themselves are all that unusual; it is the accumulation that makes the effect. The trope of surveillance may even be signaled by the first pop song, playing almost subliminally under the card game at which Joel is relating his fantasy.[6] The Police's Every Breath You Take *was a new song in 1983, a huge hit, and although commonly considered a love song, it is really a song about obsession, with the recurring refrain 'I'll be watching you'. This strand, too, comes to a head in 'In the Air Tonight' with its prominent assertion 'I saw what you did' and Joel's hyperawareness of all the eyes on them on the train.*

[143]

But the lyrics are only one signifying element of the song. In the Air Tonight' *sounds radically different from the typical pop song, both in its musical structure and its timbres (tone colour). Musically, the track lies much closer to the 'Tangerine Dream' underscore than any of the other pop songs in the score by virtue of its minimalist rhythms and the prominent voice of the synthesizer, moving in a cyclic harmonic pattern without resolution. The synth in the Phil Collins track is reedier, earthier than the ethereal 'Tangerine Dream' sound, and the 'Tangerine Dream' harmonic cycles tend to move away from tonic (the home pitch) then fall back at the beginning of the next cycle, whereas* In The Air Tonight *has a more circular shape, shifting in parallel motion - in d minor - what Phil Collins once half-jokingly called 'the saddest of all the keys' (*Face Value,*

1999), the chords are d minor-C major, Bb major, C major (i-bVII-bVI-bVII). This circular, or pendulum, cycle has less drive than the type of pattern displayed, for instance, in the 'Tangerine Dream' cue Making Love On A Real Train which follows, but it has - paradoxically - both more stability and a stronger feeling of suspense. The symmetrical balance between tonic and its closely related bVI gives the chord sequence stability, while the lack of a dominant (the chord which has the strongest polarity with tonic) gives the sequence a sliding, hazy quality.[7]

On the face of it, the song's unusual structure would seem to lend itself to the underscoring of a sexual encounter. Although vestiges of a verse-chorus format can be found, the shape is better described as a long, slow, throbbing build-up to a climactic drum break (the counterbalancing length of the rhythmic, bass-heavy out chorus is usually overshadowed by the drama of the first half). Mapping a narrative of arousal-orgasm onto the music would be an obvious strategy, but one which Risky Business - or the song itself - evades.

I Can Feel it...

Unlike the veiled stalking of Every Breath You Take (another song with an obsessively circular chord sequence), the borderline psychosis of In The Air Tonight is lyrically obvious and emphasized by the disturbing sounds of the music itself. The song is a skillfully proportioned dramatic structure, leading to the 'break'.

The recording begins with the soft, thudding rhythm of the Roland drum machine. It is mixed very low against a central spaciousness in which silence itself becomes a voice, forcing the drum machine into the background. This rhythmicised emptiness is odd, giving the listener a sense of exposure, the aural equivalent of being in a large, dark space.[8]

Example 1 The "erratic" heartbeat of the Roland drum machine

The Roland has the timbre and rhythm of an erratic heartbeat. (Example 1) It is a little faster than a resting heartbeat and has a little 'catch' at the beginning of its two-bar unit, another at the end. It is the kind of sound the body is likely to respond to empathetically, a physiological representation of mild agitation. The rhythm is also a little unsettling because in most rock music, 2 is the strongest beat in the bar; in this pattern, beat 4 has more emphasis, pulling the ear forward.

On the repetition of the 2-bar pattern, a low guitar drone enters with a rough timbre similar to that of a buzzsaw, and in bar 8, a silvery,[9] amorphous shimmer from the synthesizer precedes a two-note, two-bar wail on the guitar. So far, all the sounds are either ambiguous or encoded somehow with pain. The addition of the harmonic cycle on the organ-synth anchors the piece into a regular pattern, but it is still circular and suspended.

The lyrics are likewise circular and suspended, waiting:

I can feel it coming in the air tonight, oh, Lord...
And I've been waiting for this moment for all my life...

This is the segment of the song which might be called the chorus, but it shifts, fragments combining and recombining obsessively around the unspecified but momentous future event. The voice is a flat, edgy near-monotone with only the slightest melodic flex articulating the phrases. The rhythms are very close to those of natural English speech patterns, but continually tied across the bar-line, engaging the Roland drum machine in a subtle tension. (Example 2)

[145]

Example 2 Vocal Rhythm in the Chorus

Undercutting the final 'Oh, Lord' of the chorus is the buzzsaw guitar, intensifying its subtle threat in the following verse:

Well if you told me you were drowning,

I would not lend a hand

I've seen your face before, my friend,

but I don't know if you know who I am.

Well I was there, and I saw what you did,

I saw it with my own two eyes

So you can wipe off that grin, I know where you've been, it's all been a pack of lies!

The calm delivery and non-specific intensity of the words are betrayed by the piercing guitar and the conformity of the rhythm to the agitated Roland heartbeat. (Example 3) That subtle rhythmic shift is both a reduction of tension (the two voices are no longer in conflict) and a ratcheting up (the singer is no longer so calm).

Example 3 Vocal Rhythm in the Verse

But then the 'chorus' returns, slightly extended with the voice subjected to electronic distortion: echo at the ends of phrases and a doubling at the lower octave by a vocoder, a timbre similar to that of the buzzsaw guitar. That guitar underscores the final 'Oh, Lord' as a gathering storm of white noise sweeps forward, cresting and cutting off sharply with the first 'remember' of the next verse:

Well I remember, I remember, don't worry, (echo)

How could I ever forget, it's the first time, the last time, we ever met (echo)

But I know the reason you keep your silence up, no you don't fool me

The hurt doesn't show, but the pain still grows, it's no stranger to you and me.

The electronic distortion increases, and high, sliding vocal harmonies over the last line sound like a pinched cry of pain. This peak of intensity is capped by the thundering drum break, the rhythm a simple repeated short-long that, chained together, creates a long syncopation slamming emphatically into the last two quavers before the out chorus. (Example 4)

Example 4 Drum Break

This ferocious drum break might easily be considered cathartic. The problem with that reading is that the rhythmic and timbral distortion gets worse, not better. The extended out chorus - nearly as long as the rest of the song - may feel more stable because it doesn't have the minute fluctuations that characterize the first half of the song and the booming drums pound out on beats 2 and 4 (as is normal for rock drums). However, the rolling bassline that enters is again asymmetrical and disjunct, irregularly shaped interjections that leave 'holes' on 2 and 4 for the drums. The bassline is a four-bar pattern and syncs up every second time through the drum machine pattern, a punctuation of the end of a phrase but also a pick-up to the next repetition. This kind of overlap is not unusual for a bassline, but the amount of overlap is, emphasizing its cyclical nature. (Example 5) The guitar wails become more frequent, and Collins pushes his voice to the breaking point, the timbre splitting with the force. The sounds are deeply ingrained with pain and anger which are never assuaged.

[147]

Example 5 Bassline (after the Drum Break)

It makes the song a very strange choice for a love scene. But then, perhaps this isn't really a love scene.

Uneasy Riders

Risky Business *presents Joel and Lana as a couple, but it also knows that they are not meant for happily ever after (indeed they go their different ways at the end). Lana is actually a much more interesting character than Joel - an abused child, she has run away from home, and although she has prostituted herself, she also has a keen business sense and has learned how to fend for herself; at this point in the film, she has become assertive enough to stand up to her exploitative pimp. But like most Hollywood product, the film insists on focusing on the juvenile needs of the male lead. Perhaps there is even a trace of old-fashioned misogyny that deems Lana useful only as an aid to Joel's rite of passage - she 'makes him a man'; but since she is also a whore, she is not good enough for him as a real partner (or maybe she's an angel or deus ex machina, but either way, she's not a real woman). This dynamic, however, puts this big 'love scene' in a precarious position; yes, it is more intimate than their earlier sexual encounters - and about Lana's fantasy rather than Joel's for a change - but the focus is still on Joel's uncertainty and reaches the peak of his paranoia of surveillance. The song is not about him or his feelings, the way pop songs tend to be used narratively. Instead, the song is sung 'at him' but also through him; he projects the hostile lyrics onto the watching eyes of the other passengers on the train. 'I saw what you did' is the accusation Joel fears from the bored, tired passengers, intensified by the uneasiness of the music and the cutting and choreography of the sequence.*

None of the other pop song sequences in the film have anywhere near the integration of music and movement/editing that the In the Air Tonight *sequence does. The only one that even recognizes a relationship between the action and the non-diegetic song is the musical joke at the beginning of Jeff Beck's* The Pump, *as Joel takes his father's Porsche out of the garage for the first time. When the engine dies, the blues strut stops, then goes back to the beginning when Joel restarts the car. Most of the other songs are diegetic, and some are mixed so low, they are almost imperceptible (as in the case of* Every Breath You Take*). Even* Old-Time Rock and Roll *is more like an old-fashioned musical number: it is quite emphatically diegetic, as the scene starts with Joel shoving all the sliders on his father's equalizer to the top; Joel's movements are miming and dancing, and the editing is, for the most part, simply cut to the beat. It is fun,[10] but it lacks the cinematic nuance of* In the Air Tonight.

The music begins with a short montage of bored, sleepy prostitutes and Joel's friend and fellow 'Future Enterpriser' Barry (Bronson Pinchot) (the gay sidekick?) counting the money under Joel's narration about the success of their bordello. A shot of a car being pushed across the dark screen coincides with the entry of the keyboard, a kind of visual analog to the slow motion of the chord sequence, as well as a kinetic foreshadowing of the train, which always runs left to right on the screen. Lana and Joel go to a diner,[11] and Joel's voiceover relates Lana's desire to 'make love on a real train'. 'Who was I to argue?' he asks as the scene changes to the turnstiles of the train station, cuing the entry of the lyrics, 'I can feel it coming in the air tonight.' At this stage, the music merely seems anticipatory, but the edit comes at an odd point, neither on the beat nor off of it, and similarly, the doors of the train open just after the first 'oh, Lord' - but too quickly, a jarring rhythm. Throughout the first part of the song, up to the drum break, all the edits are like this, arrhythmic, unsettling, like an extension of the agitated rhythm of the song itself. Some of the movements in frame, however, 'catch' the music in unexpected synchrony.

Joel and Lana get on the train and the camera pulls back as the doors shut on the final words of 'I've been waiting for this moment for all my life,' a gesture which seems oddly final - in another context, it might be seen as symbolic of death, combining the closing of the doors on 'my life' with the cinematic cliché of ending and departure, the pull-back. Another 'displaced' edit takes us inside the train, and the lights suddenly go out on 'can't you feel it'. Joel whispers urgently, 'You said no one was gonna be here,' and Lana soothes him with a caress of her hand over his back, but as her hand continues down to squeeze his buttock, the action is underlined by the entry of the buzzsaw guitar under 'Oh, Lord!'

A shot of a disapproving woman cuts to Joel and Lana sitting on a bench seat, legs entwined, via another dimming of the lights, which come back up on the white-noise crest at 'I remember!' Collins sings, 'don't worry,' and Lana again soothes Joel with a caress, and there is another unsettling edit right before 'how could I ever forget', to another blackout and a shot of people's backs as they go down the aisle of the train.

On the sweep up to 'the last time we ever met,' Lana grabs Joel and pulls him into a hungry kiss, though he is highly uncomfortable, aware of being watched. 'But I know why you keep your silence up,' cuts to a shot of a bored wino yawning, strongly suggesting that Joel's paranoia is just that, but Joel cringes back against the windows on 'the pain still grows', and Lana leans forward against him, 'It's no stranger to you and me!' Joel's eyes cut toward the wino (Steve - this is the image I want!) as the drums thunder in; the bum eats something, still bored.

Just as the music is irrevocably changed by the entry of the drums and the bass, so is the editing style. Now, the editing falls solidly within the rhythmic structure of the song. The train pulls into a station with the entry of the bass (echoing the earlier shot of the car), and the doors open on the buzzsaw guitar; they shut on beat 2, the strongest beat of the bar and in the gap of the bassline. Lana strokes the back of her hand against Joel's chest on 'I've been waiting for this moment for all my life,' and Joel's final look at the wino leads to him taking this last passenger off the train. The song fades out rather suddenly, and the depositing of the wino on a bench at a station takes place in an unexpected silence. Back on the train, Tangerine Dream's pulsating cue fades up and the music-video-style sex scene begins, but musically it is all an anti-climax.

[149]

Clean Reading

On superficial hearing, the song's structure would seem to offer itself up all too easily to a sex scene. If that was the intention, then the film was spectacularly unsuccessful: the editing is incompetent and the temporal vectors of the two dramatic structures (agitated drum machine to ferocious drum break/foreplay to orgasm) fail to coincide. But such a crashing mistake would seem unlikely.

Instead, the sequence attempts something far more subtle. The song is not just its unusual structure. The tension within its rhythmic texture and the anguished timbres makes it unsettling and even threatening. The vagueness of its lyrics gives it flexibility and ambiguity, but there is also a remarkable tendency to want to 'tie it down' to some concrete meaning, whether it is the urban legend that the song is about Collins watching someone die or the baffling, unexplained reasoning which led the BBC to ban the song during the Gulf War - the song likewise, and just as inexplicably, made the infamous 'don't play-list' for American radio in the wake of September 11.

The very free-floating anxiety of the song makes it powerfully symbolic of the adolescent unease demonstrated throughout the film. When the lyrics' accusatory 'I saw what you did' activates the trope of surveillance, the resonance is deeper. The scene pulls all the major threads of the film together - Joel's rites of passage (emotional, educational, and sexual), the train imagery, the various plot lines - for the only time in the film. The music is even closer in style to the underscore than the rest of the pop songs.

That said, this may not be a reading that would be grasped easily. It might actually be easier for audiences to understand it on the level at which it fails - the blatant sexual level. It is an intriguing problem. Would that failure in any way niggle at the subconscious of an audience which tries to make it work at that level? Might there be a subliminal understanding of the way all the symbolic and narrative filaments pass through this scene? Yet even that reading is a little unsatisfying, musically if nothing else - the song is faded out rather abruptly after the false catharsis of the drum break.

It is hard to get a good grasp - a clean reading, as it were - of the scene. Nothing about it is comfortable, even when it seems to 'work' on a symbolic level. But then, the song itself is 'uncomfortable'. Perhaps this bad fit is actually appropriate, more expressive of the song's content and its intersection with the film than a correlation that 'works' on all levels.

Risky Business *was a hit, and its soundtrack, coming as it did alongside* Flashdance, *was a landmark in cross-marketing strategy. But* In the Air Tonight *became something much bigger in popular culture during the decade that followed. A little over a year later, the song was used in the pilot episode of the massive cultural phenomenon* Miami Vice. *Here, the song was also poised at the dramatic and emotional peak of the narrative (one might also ponder how much the power of the song itself creates the feeling that this is, indeed, the peak of the narrative). Likewise, there was more than one layer operating - what was coming 'in the air tonight' was a showdown with the villain; but the 'remember' verse was wound poignantly around a tentative conversation between Sonny Crockett and his estranged wife. Here, the symbolic balance is shifted to the lyrics, reinterpreting their meaning in a new context, whereas in* Risky Business, *the emphasis is primarily on the sound of the song. (See Stilwell, 1995, for a more extensive analysis) The song was used in the extensive television campaign promoting the new show, and also became the only one ever to be used twice in the television series, appearing in the pre-title teaser sequence of the show's flashback episode* A Bullet for Crockett, *where the build to the drum break coincides with Crockett being shot - the kind of parallel vectorization that doesn't* happen in Risky Business, *but also a more superficial incidence, unless one considers the intratextual link that the song has within the series. The song even revisited the charts in the fall of 1984, on the heels of Collins's summer smash hit* Against All Odds *(another cross-promotion, from the film of the same name) and just preceding the release of Collins's smash album* No Jacket Required.

Even before his breakthrough, Collins had been deeply involved with the Prince's Trust charity in Britain, appearing in numerous concerts and even the film The Secret Policeman's Other Ball *(1982), playing* In the Air Tonight *on the piano - he sheepishly admitted later that it was one of the few songs of his he could actually play on the piano, and therefore perform solo. This version was another life altogether for a song which, for most people, existed primarily as a highly mediated electronic recording. Stripped down to the acoustic piano and voice, however, the song did seem to retain its haunting power for audiences, and it became a staple of the many high profile charity concerts of the 1980s, not least LiveAid, where it (along with* Against All Odds, *another song Collins could play on the piano - this one in Db) became the only song played in both London and Philadelphia. The extent to which this song - never a major chart hit in the US - had become widely absorbed into popular culture was demonstrated in Philadelphia when Collins, as was usual in acoustic performances, left a silence where the drum break should have been. The audience roared out the drum break for him - not the same thing as singing along with a catchy chorus, but demonstrating a much deeper understanding of the dramatic structure of the song.*

[151]

These were only the most prominent manifestations of the song. Its video was itself very popular on MTV and rated very highly on polls of 'greatest videos' right to the end of the decade, unusual for a relatively primitive early video, though one rich with symbolism. The song was one of those used in the infamous The Night Belongs to Michelob *series of beer commercials in the late 1980s, which sparked heated debate about 'selling out' among journalists (though, similarly to its use in* Risky Business, *the song seemed to slough off attempts to make it signify a sexual encounter, and it was probably the least successful of the ads, as evidenced by its relatively short broadcast life). It featured in at least one American soap opera (*Guiding Light, *1982), and was the signature tune for Virgin Records' 25th Anniversary celebration television special and recording compilation in 1994, even though it was not Virgin's most successful single, or even its first hit.*

This wide cultural propagation puts In the Air Tonight *in* Risky Business *in a position that is, if not unique, at least unusually prominent. It highlights a problem rarely considered when dealing with intertextuality and pop songs in film. Most of the time, we scholars talk about what the meaning of the song was to the audience of the film when it was released. But what happens if the song becomes more popular* after *the film is released, and yet this cinematic moment is one of the 'lesser' occurrences of the song? In this context, 'clean reading' has less to do with a secure grasp on the reading - as it does within the text of* Risky Business - *than it does with the more obvious meaning of a reading free of 'contamination'.*

Certainly, In the Air Tonight *is not remembered for* Risky Business *nearly so much as it is for* Miami Vice *or the acoustic concert performances. It may be that familiarity with the other uses of the song would produce a bored shrug, 'Oh, yeah, yeah, slow build up, drum break - been there, done that.' It might blunt a more active generation of meaning in which the listening/viewing subject worries at the 'problem' of the song in the film's context. Or perhaps it would lead the subject to a different expectation - the* Miami Vice *examples might cause one to anticipate violence rather than sex; in that case the odd anticlimax of bundling the wino onto the bench in silence might be doubly disappointing or frustrating. Or the conflation of* Miami Vice *and* Risky Business *could alert the subject to a wider, historical awareness of the aesthetics of the early MTV era. In any case - unless the subject is so young that s/he is completely innocent of the song's pop-cultural status - the reading is highly unlikely to be the same as that original audience's.*

Contamination can also be enrichment. Perhaps a clean reading is a sterile one.

Notes

1   *In his excellent The Sounds of Commerce (1998), Jeff demonstrates that although this configura-tion is new-and the boom in video rental will add a new spoke to the wheel very shortly-cross-pro-motion between the film and music industries is hardly new (in part because they have never been wholly separate entities).*

2   *Accusations that MTV was offering free advertising for films through these videos (particularly "Maniac" from Flashdance) eventually led to a demand that the sequence be recut to feature at least 50% of Bob Seger in concert (Smith 1998: 201).*

3   *The only established song in the latter film was Joan Jett's "I Love Rock and Roll", which was left off the soundtrack for licensing reasons.*

4   *Elsewhere (Stilwell 1995), I have traced the various guises of the song from the original video through the 1980s and up to its enshrinement as the signature song for Virgin Records' 25th anniversary in 1994.*

5   *The development of polyphonic keyboard synthesizers and their sudden drop in price around 1980 made the synth score especially attractive to low-budget films, and since a large proportion of low-budget films can be categorized as horror or fantasy, one could argue that it is merely coincidence that the connection occurs. It is true, too, that economy was a factor in the choice of synthesizer*

for Mark Snow's score for *The X-Files* television series *(1993-2002)*. However,, the "magical" sound of the synthesizer is still brought to bear even in the period fantasy of *The Natural* (Barry Levinson, 1984), and is particularly amenable to blending with sound effect, as in the scores of Brad Fiedel (*The Terminator* (James Cameron, 1984), *The Terminator 2: Judgment Day* (James Cameron, 1991), and *Blue Steel* (Kathryn Bigelow, 1990), for example). This blending also lends itself to a suspension of reality, a kind of fantastical atmosphere.

6   Watching this film on video, I was only cued to the song's presence by the list of copyright acknowledgements in the end credits. It took repeated viewings at high volume to "find" the song. One does have to question whether it was audible in the original theatrical audio mix. But other questions arise: Why pick such a popular song and then have it mixed down so far? Was it meant to be subliminal, relying on its very popularity so that people recognized it on some level without realizing it? Is the very fact that it is barely audible yet still there a cue to its symbolic import?

7   In technical terms, the sequence is modal rather than tonal, and that difference often evokes ambiguity and a kind of antiquity to most listeners. This particular chord sequence is not an uncommon one in 1970s rock, particularly in serious or brooding contexts (for instance, Kansas's "Wayward Son").

8   One may be reminded of Julia Kristeva's chora, a womb-like but chaotic space which orders the basic drives and manifests flashes of energy and rhythm. (1984/1997: 52) I am not actually convinced by all of Kristeva's argument, but the paradoxically nurturing/seductive and threatening space does seem an apt description of that created by both "In the Air Tonight" and the train-sex scene in *Risky Business*.

[153]

9   There is no technical language available for timbre, one of the most important qualities in jazz and rock music; we are forced to rely on synesthetic adjectives, most often visual or tactile analogies.

10 The undeniable erotics (particularly the homoerotics) of this scene are clearly significant, but would really require another chapter to deal with.

11 There is an interesting similarity between this point and a similar point in the song's more famous use in the pilot episode of *Miami Vice*-the prominence of a neon sign. Perhaps it is just part of the stylistic palette of 1980s pop culture, but perhaps there is a kind of subliminal cue in the buzzing timbre of the guitar drone and the buzz and glow of a neon sign. Maybe I'm pushing it.

References

Collins, Phil. (1999), *Classic Albums: Face Value*. Imagine Entertainment DVD.

Kristeva, Julia. (1984, *Revolution in Poetic Language.* Translated by Margaret Waller. New York: Columbia Press. Reprinted in Kelly Oliver (Ed.) *The Portable Kristeva*. New York: Columbia University Press, 1997, pp. 27-69.

Smith, Jeff. (1998), The Sounds of Commerce: Marketing Popular Film Music, New York: Columbia University Press.

Stilwell, Robynn J. (1995) "In the Air Tonight': Text, Intertextuality, and the Creation of Meaning,' *Popular Music and Society* 19:3, pp. 67-103.

Falling Into Coma: Wong Kar Wei and Massive Attack *David Toop*

Karma Coma [Massive Attack, 1994] / Fallen Angels [Wong Kar Wei, 1992]

Falling Into Coma: Wong Kar-Wai and Massive Attack

David Toop

Typically, pop song intersects the logic of film as a hiatus. The enveloping illusion of cinema is overlaid with a secondary illusion, determined by the lyric of the song. Cinema time is suspended, replaced temporarily by the alien time of the song. In a Wong Kar-Wai film, that relationship is different. An interlocking takes place, through which the song becomes an invisible character, enmeshed within the complex ambient soundscape of its contextual scene yet utterly plausible as a transferable inner voice.

Often compared with the young Jean-Luc Godard, Wong Kar-Wai is celebrated as one of the leading auteurs of new wave Asian cinema. 'Wong may be said to have brought the Hong Kong new wave into the 90s,' wrote Stephen Teo, 'by combining post-modern themes with new wave stylistics.' Born in Shanghai in 1958, he moved to Hong Kong with his family at the age of five. His father ran a nightclub in the Tsimshatsui district, a club called The Bayside where The Beatles gave a press conference during their Far Eastern tour of 1965. Many scenes in a Wong Kar-Wai film are saturated with apparent nostalgia for the Hong Kong of this period. 'This film is more personal to me,' he told Jonathan Romney in conversation prior to the release of In The Mood For Love. *'It's about a certain period in our life, a certain lifestyle or manner that is already lost.'*

Popular songs are central to this theme of loss. The title of Wong Kar-Wai's first film - As Tears Go By *(1988) - was taken from Marianne Faithfull's 1964 hit single of the same name, whilst the film itself drew heavily on Martin Scorsese's* Mean Streets, *itself a significant marker of the use of pop songs in cinema. The title of* Happy Together *(1998) was taken from the record by The Turtles. Speaking to Richard Williams about this film, Wong Kar-Wai discussed the way in which we hear music in an urban environment. Implicit in his observations is the idea that this unpredictable soundtrack creates an invisible architecture, an emotional backdrop that contributes strongly to subjective experiences of the city: 'I spent two months in Beijing. It made me want to make a film there, because I saw how strange it is. Every night, around six or seven o'clock, we'd leave the studio and go back to our hotel. We'd take a cab, and the radio station would be playing jazz. It was very strange to hear John Coltrane in Tiananmen Square, in a programme sponsored by Maxwell House coffee. But, you know, this was exactly what I felt when I moved to Hong Kong when I was five. The sound of the city was quite different from what I had known in Shanghai. So I thought, well, now's the time to make a film of Beijing.'*

In Chungking Express *(1994),* California Dreamin *by The Mamas and Papas functions not just as a replacement for dialogue but as the core message of the film. 'In* Chungking Express,*' writes*

Larry Gross, California Dreamin *is played some nine or ten times almost in its entirety. But only towards the end do you grasp that dancing casually to that song and letting its lyric play across your mind is almost literally what the movie is about. His world is very much the world with a soundtrack, where objects - perishable but still emotionally resonant - flit in and out of our hands and minds.'*

In the absence of an outer voice, the song articulates the obsession with time common to all characters in a Wong Kar-Wai film: what is passing or lost; what might be possible in the idealised future; can decisions and actions be measured in the same way that a sell-buy date measures the freshness of a tin of pineapples? A telling scene in Fallen Angels *shows one of the main characters shooting video of his father. They have little verbal communication despite living in the same small hotel room: the son is mute; the father rarely talks since the death of his wife. The son's persistence with his video camera becomes so unbearable that his father shuts him out of their room. Later, he is filmed asleep. In private moments he watches these videos with pleasure and after his death, his son watches one sequence over and over, relishing the pleasure of a rare smile from his father.*

The role of electronic media in memory, when one-to-one communication is difficult or thwarted, is a theme that recurs throughout Wong Kar-Wai's films. When characters are mute, inarticulate, or emotionally withdrawn, songs animate their silence. Fallen Angels *(1995) begins with a long sequence in which voices are heard only as peripheral chatter or voiceover. Preceding the main titles is a scene shot in black and white; the hit man, Wong Chi-Ming (played by Leon Lai) and his agent (played by Michele Reis) are discussing their professional and personal relationship: 'Are we still partners?' she asks from the foreground of the shot. We see her cigarette shaking. 'Three years as business partners but we've never sat together before,' he replies, a smudged figure in the background. 'We rarely meet. It's hard for a man to control his passion, so we shouldn't get involved.' This neurotic, internalised, literally colourless fragment is then swept aside by a tour de force of camerawork, set design, sound and conceptualisation, sustained without dialogue or exposition for nearly ten minutes.*

[157]

Films that open with such bravado inevitably owe a debt to Touch of Evil, *directed in 1958 by Orson Welles. There are signs, perhaps illusory, that Wong Kar-Wai was influenced by this infamous sequence in more than just ambition.* Touch Of Evil *begins with a lengthy uninterrupted tracking shot that follows the progress of narcotics agent Charlton Heston and his new bride, played by Janet Leigh, as they arrive in a Mexican border town for their honeymoon. Cars glide across shot as they move through the streets. A powerful mood of urban excitement, verging on chaos, dominates the sequence, underlined by Henry Mancini's percussive Latin theme. The climax of the scene is an explosion.*

The arc is similar. The first non-vocal sound we hear in Fallen Angels *is a brief drum break, recognisable as one of the 'hooks' from Massive Attack's* Karmacoma. *Shot from a variety of angles, the agent is walking through an underground subway, moving on escalators. Immediately, the drums mesh with a common experience of walking through such empty, connective and threatening urban spaces: the amplified sounds of footsteps echoing in an uncomfortable silence. The agent is heading for a tiny, extremely basic apartment. We quickly learn that this barren home belongs to the hit man. Improbably, the agent starts to clean his room. She puts on a white mask, turns on the television, and energetically starts to smooth his bed covers, scrub the floor, replenish the fridge with beer. A large clock is caught in a flash of white light. Outside, trains roar past, streaking the sky with lines of light.*

Rapid programme changes heard from the television (we see it as a flickering globe of light, or in extreme close-up, capturing the moment of an IBM advert) denote passing time: we hear fragments of music and voices, then part of a documentary on the Vietnam War. We gather a sense of the outside world, its chaos and fragmentation, a bizarre reality check for the equally strange, hermetic relationship of the hit man and the agent. A strong atmosphere of repressed sexuality emerges through the eroticism of this scene. Often on all fours and in a role of voluntary servitude in this oppressively masculine environment, the agent wears a tight black plastic dress and fishnet stockings. Since the hit man is not present we can only imagine that this slightly old-fashioned uniform of soft-core pornography represents a fantasy of the agent (as the opening dialogue suggests, and later scenes make explicit, her desire and love for the hit man is unrequited).

This scene cuts to a shot of the hit man walking through what may be the same pristine, ultra-modern subway. His footsteps echo and merge with the Karmacoma *beats. We see that the surroundings of his apartment are run-down; observing him in long shot, from outside, we hear the trains, a hysterical passage of police sirens, car horns, and traffic. Inside the room, the ubiquitous TV obliterates lonely silence. Wong sleeps on top of his carefully smoothed bed, television sound yammering around the edges of his coma.*

The agent leaves a coded answer machine message: 'A message for 3662. I'll visit those friends tomorrow. Where and when?' Next we see her in a gambling club. Her voiceover exposes her isolation from human contact, her mute behaviour in the club is underlined by a feeling of craziness created by Cantonese pop and Christopher Doyle's continually disorientating camera work. Initially, she looks drunk and unsteady, then belligerent. In slow motion, wearing a leopard skin top, she exits to the sound of Karmacoma. *Transcendent with cool, mysterious, impossibly beautiful, her face is almost totally obscured by a mane of black hair. The conscious exoticism of this moment interlocks with the exotic musical undercurrent of* Karmacoma.

We see her back in her room, drawing a plan of the club. The television is on, playing a bizarre, hectic mix of records. She faxes him the plan; in long shot, we see him receive the fax. The sound design segues from Hong Kong pop music into train sounds into the sound of a money counting machine in her room. She is all professionalism yet wracked with desire. The scene cuts to the hit man, setting off for the same club. As is the case throughout this long sequence, it is night. Apparently, these characters only live in shadow and the artificial light of neon, televisions and underground halogen. We hear the sound of a siren that blends into the first beats of 'Karmacoma'. Ambient sounds are heard only sporadically. We seem to be observing actions set within an acoustically sealed bubble. There is a moment when we hear his footsteps, sharp as drum beats or gunshots on the hard floor, then the 'silence' returns with Karmacoma. *His hand points down, perfectly cut to the beat; he draws his guns and the music is abruptly replaced by the sound of shooting. The killing is explosive, orgiastic. Bodies fall in all directions, blood spatters the camera lens (as if we are literal voyeurs of all this carnage) and as the last shot is fired, the music is mixed back in. He leaves, pushing aside a plastic curtain that cracks as loudly as a cannon shot. Briefly, moans of the dying can be heard, then silence. As he jumps onto a bus to make his escape, normal (in other words, located in context and narrative) sound is heard for the first time. This abrupt transition is completed by the farcical tone of the scene, as the hit man is recognised by an old school friend who tries to sell him insurance. 'Even a hit man has a past,' the hit man muses, though in the tradition of Clint Eastwood or Alain Delon in* Le Samourai, *he says nothing. We hear his unspoken thoughts in voiceover.*

[159]

The length and obscurity of this opening sequence is extraordinary. For ten minutes, little is said and nothing is explained except through rapid editing, the juxtaposition of symbolic imagery, sound and music, the backdrop of the city. There are numerous echoes of Ridley Scott's Blade Runner, *though a closer parallel can be found in Asian cinema. Akira Kurosawa's* Stray Dog, *made in Japan in 1949, tells the story of a policeman, Murakami (played by Toshiro Mifune), whose gun is stolen during an intensely hot post-war Tokyo summer. Determined to get his pistol back, he searches the black-market district until he finds the thief. In a strikingly original sequence we watch him walk through the black-market of Ueno in search of clues. There are no words; only ambient sounds and a montage of popular songs, many of them Japanese versions of Hawaiian or Cuban music.*

'This sequence runs for nearly ten minutes,' writes Stuart Galbraith IV in The Emperor and The Wolf: The Lives and Films of Akira Kurosawa and Toshiro Mifune, *'and has been criticized as excessive.' 'The atmosphere is caught, to be sure,' wrote Donald Richie, '...but it is so long that one expects summer to be over and autumn begun by the time it finally stops. But this long, exhilarating sequence does more than simply capture post-war Tokyo and black-market seaminess. Its length comes close to the breaking point because it needs to. Murakami's*

determination must exceed our own; the montage serves to illustrate this, while putting the audience inside his very psyche.'

A similar claim could be made for the sequence that begins Fallen Angels. *Wong Kar-Wai constantly returns to sounds and images of communication and movement in the city - trains, cars, escalators, TVs, radios, answer machines, faxes, money - yet the two central protagonists are locked into a relationship of stunted communications. Their loneliness verges on hysteria. Release comes for the hit man through killing; for his agent, through masturbation. Their world is bounded by communications - both literally and symbolically - and in this sea of movement, their lives appear distressingly fluid, appallingly empty.*

Wong Kar-Wai and his crew build this image with a dazzling array of techniques: Chris Doyle's cinematography, William Chang's production design, Cheng Xialong's sound effects and Leung Tat's sound recording. All of these techniques contribute to a feeling of perpetual instability and alienation. We are rarely close to the characters, even in their most intimate confessional moments, yet our distance - physical and emotional - fluctuates all the time. There is no centre in Wong Kar-Wai's films, no character or point of view so firmly placed that we can identify with a personality or a moral stance. We sit on the outside, entranced by the glamour and wretched pathos of loneliness: the endless cigarettes, the self-justification, the nihilism.

[160]

Central to this mood is Massive Attack's Karmacoma. *But of course, nothing is central in a Wong Kar-Wai film. Very quickly we question the authenticity of this* Karmacoma. *Is it a remix we don't know (very possible, since Massive Attack are famous for their creative and sometimes obscure remixes)? Questions abound on Wong Kar-Wai websites and the answers are vague. One fan asks if the track is* Bumper Ball Dub, *taken from the Massive Attack V. Mad Professor dub album with an added Cantonese vocal. A vocal can be heard during the hit man's walk to the first killing, an indecipherable mumble that is subtitled to reveal the hit mans' philosophy of life: he's a loner, he's lazy, he likes his job because there are no decisions. Somebody he doesn't know decides that somebody else has to die. In all senses, he executes the job. Only two words are clear - 'I'm cool'. The mumble could be Cantonese or deep Jamaican patois. Hard to tell.*

Karmacoma *is perfect for this context, since its origins, its versions and its meanings are thoroughly convoluted. Composed by the members of Massive Attack, along with another Bristol based musician, Tricky, the track appeared on Massive Attack's hugely successful* Protection *album, released in 1994. The vocals were taken by Robert '3D' Del Naja and Tricky. Another version, titled* Overcome, *appeared on Tricky's remarkable debut album of 1995,* Maxinquaye. *Massive Attack's version was also released as a single, which appeared in a number of remixes. As for* Fallen Angels, *a new version was created by musical directors Frankie Chan and Roel A. Garcia.*

The atmosphere created by Massive Attack and Tricky fits the film extremely well, being glamorous, mysterious, culturally ambiguous, melancholy and somewhat paranoid. This is a music of fractured emotional lives negotiating alienated urban spaces. The sound seems to grow organically from echoing underground car parks and subways, alarms and passing traffic, its rumbling bass speaking for the undertow of urban night. Saturated by the influence of Jamaican dub, a mixing technique that transforms an original source through echoes and other effects, Massive Attack's music mirrors the dub camerawork of Doyle. Just as every echo delay in the music undergoes a subtle difference, every view seen through Doyle's lens has a variation of colour, texture, speed or angle.

Though never heard in the film, the opening lyric of the original track offers a clue to the attraction of this song for Wong Kar-Wai: 'You sure you wanna be with me? I've nothing to give.' There lies the tale of the hit man and his agent. Discussing Wong Kar-Wai's second film, Days Of Being Wild, *Stephen Teo has written: 'The associations of the characters are built up through a kind of narrative puzzle: each character is a connective piece.'* Fallen Angels *offers a further development of this method, in which a part of the puzzle can only be accessed through knowledge of the song that pulses at the heart of its soundtrack.*

References

Galbraith IV, S. (2001), *The Emperor and The Wolf*. New York & London: Faber and Faber.

Gross, L. (1996) 'Nonchalant Grace' in *Sight and Sound*, September.

Romney, J. (2000)'Mood Music', *The Guardian*, October 23.

Massive Attack, (1994), *Protection*, Circa Records wbrcd2.

Massive Attack V. (1995), *Mad Professor*, Circa records wbrcd3.

Teo, S. (1997), *Hong Kong Cinema: The Extra Dimensions,* BFI Publishing.

Tricky, M. (1995), *Island BRCD* 610.

Williams, R. (1998), 'King Kong', *The Guardian*, April 10.

Contributors

Dave Beech was a prominent member of the young London art scene in the mid-90's, working with BANK. He has had solo shows at Flag gallery (London), The Trade Apartment (London), Sparwasser HQ (Berlin), Collective Gallery (Edinburgh) as well as important group exhibitions such as Futurology at the New Art Gallery Walsall, Radio Radio at International 3, (Manchester), Strike in (Wolverhampton and Philadelphia), Nanoscopic Culture, (London) and Slimvolume. He is a regular writer for Art Monthly *and other art magazines and was the co-author of the* Verso anthology The Philistine Controversy. *He also edited a special issue of* Third Text *entitled* Art, Politics and Resistance.

Matthew Caley is Senior Lecturer in Graphic Communication, School Of Art & Design at The University Of Wolverhampton. As a poet his first collection Thirst *[Slow Dancer, 1999] was nominated for The Forward Prize For Best First Collection. His second,* The Scene Of My Former Triumph *is forthcoming from Wrecking Ball.*

Elizabeth Caldwell Hirschman is Professor II of Marketing in the School of Business, Rutgers University, USA. Her research interests include semiotics, cultural anthropology, hedonic consumption, ethnicity and archetypic imagery. She has written over 200 research articles and papers, authored several books on interpretive methods and, most recently, published a book examining the archetypal development of the top fifty motion pictures and top 35 television programs Heroes, Monsters, and Messiahs: The Mythology of Motion Pictures and Television, *(Andrews McMeel publishing, 2000).*

Morris B. Holbrook is the W. T. Dillard Professor of Marketing in the Graduate School of Business at Columbia University. Since 1975, he has taught courses at the Columbia Business School in such areas as Marketing Strategy, Consumer Behavior, and Commercial Communication in the Culture of Consumption. His research has covered a wide variety of topics in marketing and consumer behavior with a special focus on issues related to communication in general and to aesthetics, semiotics, hermeneutics, art, entertainment, music, motion pictures, nostalgia, and stereography in particular. Recent books include The Semiotics of Consumption *(with Elizabeth C. Hirschman, Mouton de Gruyter, 1993);* Consumer Research *(Sage, 1995); and* Consumer Value *(edited, Routledge, 1999).*

Ian Inglis is Senior Lecturer in Sociology at the University of Northumbria. He is a member of the editorial board of Popular Music & Society, *and has published widely in a variety of books and journals. His doctoral research considered the significance of sociological, social psychological, and cultural theory in explanations of the career of the Beatles. His books include* The Beatles,

Popular Music And Society: A Thousand Voices *(Macmillan 2000);* Popular Music And Film *(Wallflower 2003);* Performance and Popular Music: History, Place And Time *(Ashgate 2005).*

Anahid Kassabian is Associate Professor and Co-Director of the Literary Studies Program at Fordham University, [where she also serves on the Women's Studies Program Faculty]. She has published widely in film and popular music studies, including Hearing Film: Tracking Identification in Contemporary Hollywood Film Music *(New York and London: Routledge, 2001)] and* Keeping Score: Music, Disciplinarity, Culture *[(co-edited with David Schwarz; University Press of Virginia, 1997)].*

Steve Lannin is Senior Lecturer in Graphic Design at the Southampton Institute, University College. He has professional interests in Corporate Branding and Audio-Visual Design, acting as a consultant to Corporate Sound, Switzerland. A varied background of previous work includes: a series of songs published by Oval Music, London; illustrated works ranging from Oxford University Press Manuscripts to Gay Times *editorials; has contributed to* eye, Zingmagazine, New York *and in 2000 gave the paper "Audio Branding in the Urban Environment" at the UK's first audio-branding seminar 'No!se', hosted by the Design Council, London.*

Miguel Mera is Senior Lecturer in Composition for Screen at the Royal College of Music. He has published widely on screen music-related subjects including humour in film music, the boundary between music and sound-design and the portrayal of historical period in film music. Forthcoming publications include a jointly edited volume on European Film Music *(Ashgate),* Mychael Danna's The Ice Storm: A Film Score Study Guide *(Scarecrow Press) and* Takemitsu's Composed Space in Kurosawa's Ran *in* Film Music Reader *(CUP). Miguel also composes music for film, television and theatre, his recent work including scores for independent film production companies, Channel 4, Channel 5, the Royal Shakespeare Company, Regent's Park Theatre, and Youth Music Theatre U.K. He also serves on the BAFTA Events and Education Committee.*

Phil Powrie is Professor of French Cultural Studies at the University of Newcastle upon Tyne. He has published widely in French cinema studies, including French Cinema in the 1980s: Nostalgia and the Crisis of Masculinity *(Oxford University Press, 1997),* Contemporary French Cinema: Continuity and Difference *(editor, Oxford University Press, 1999),* Jean-Jacques Beineix *(Manchester University Press, 2001),* French Cinema: An Introduction *(co-author, Arnold, 2002), and* 24 Frames: French Cinema *(editor, Wallflower Press, 2005). He has co-edited* The Trouble with Men: Masculinities in European and Hollywood Cinema *(Wallflower Press, 2004),* Changing Tunes: The Use of Pre-existing Music in Film *(Ashgate, forthcoming 2005), and* Composing for the Screen in the USSR and Germany *(Indiana University Press, forthcoming 2006).*

John Roberts is a writer. He is the author of a number of books including: The Art of Interruption: Realism, Photography and the Everyday*(MUP, 1998) and the editor of* Art has no history! : the making and unmaking of modern art*(Verso, 1994). He has also contributed to a number of journals and magazines including:* New Left Review, Radical Philosophy, Oxford Art Journal, Cabinet *and* Historical Materialism. *His latest book (co-authored with Dave Beech) is* The Philistine Controversy *(Verso, 2002).*

Jeff Smith an Associate Professor and the Director of the Program in Film and Media Studies at Washington University in St. Louis. He is the author of The Sounds of Commerce: Marketing Popular Music. *He is currently at work on an essay about Richard Linklater's School of Rock for the online journal,* Senses of the Cinema.

David Toop is a composer and author. He has published four books: Rap Attack, Ocean Of Sound, Exotica, *and* Haunted Weather. *He has written for many publications, including* The Wire, The Face, The Times, The New York Times, Urb *and* Bookforum. *In 2000, he curated Sonic Boom, the UK's biggest exhibition of sound art, for the Hayward Gallery in London and in 2001 he curated sound for Radical Fashion at the Victoria & Albert Museum. His first album was released on Brian Eno's Obscure label in 1975 and since 1995 he has released seven solo CDs. At Lisbon Expo '98 he composed the music for the nightly spectacular, Acqua Matrix. He is currently an AHRB Research Fellow in the Creative and Performing Arts.*

[165]

Index